PARADISE & EZRA POUND

The Poet as Shaman

Scott Eastham

UNIVERSITY
PRESS OF
AMERICA

75874

LANHAM • NEW YORK • LONDON

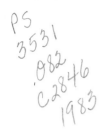

Copyright © 1983 by

University Press of America,™ Inc.

4720 Boston Way
Lanham, MD 20706

3 Henrietta Street
London WC2E 8LU England

Library of Congress Cataloging in Publication Data

Eastham, Scott, 1949–
  Paradise & Ezra Pound.

    Bibliography: p.
    1. Pound, Ezra, 1885-1972. Cantos. 2. Pound, Ezra,
1885-1972–Religion and ethics. 3. Paradise in literature.
4. Shamanism in literature. I. Title. II. Title: Paradise and
Ezra Pound.
PS3531.082C2846   1983   811'.52   83-10243
ISBN 0-8191-3370-1
ISBN 0-8191-3371-X (pbk.)

This book is dedicated
to Alice & Harry Hirsch,
my most esteemed Elders,
who first taught me:
"that the truth
is in kindness." (EP/CXIV)

ACKNOWLEDGMENTS

Excerpts from the following works of Ezra Pound are reprinted here with the permission of New Directions Publishing Corporation:

THE CANTOS OF EZRA POUND - Copyright © 1934, 1937, 1940, 1948, 1956, 1959, 1962, 1963, 1966, 1968 by Ezra Pound; Copyright © 1972 by The Estate of Ezra Pound.

PERSONAE - Copyright © 1926 by Ezra Pound.

TRANSLATIONS - Copyright © 1954, 1963 by Ezra Pound. All rights reserved.

GAUDIER-BRZESKA, A Memoir - Copyright © 1970 by Ezra Pound. All rights reserved.

GUIDE TO KULCHUR - Copyright © 1970 by Ezra Pound. All rights reserved.

SELECTED PROSE 1909-1965 - Copyright © 1973 by The Estate of Ezra Pound.

WOMEN OF TRACHIS - Copyright © 1957 by Ezra Pound.

LITERARY ESSAYS - Copyright © 1918, 1920, 1935.

THE SPIRIT OF ROMANCE - Copyright © 1968 by Ezra Pound. All rights reserved.

CONFUCIUS - Copyright © 1947, 1950 by Ezra Pound.

The author would also like to thank the following for permission to quote extracts from copyrighted sources:

Hugh Kenner, The Pound Era, Berkeley (University of California Press) 1971.

Herbert Fingarette, Confucius - The Secular as Sacred, New York (Harper & Row) 1972.

Macmillan Publishing Co., W. B. Yeats, A Vision, New York/London (Macmillan) 1937.

PARADISE & EZRA POUND

-- The Poet As Shaman

By Scott Eastham

CONTENTS   PAGE

PROLOGUE

Religion & Literature;

A Note on Method

A Man(1) speaks: The lower jaw wobbles, the lips
purse, the tongue wags, and the vocal cords hum as a
puff of air is expelled from the lungs. A sound
issues from the mouth, coupled with a gesture and
perhaps a knowing glance. A "word" is formed... but
what does it mean, what does it say to us? Not much
so far, not on the surface anyway. Unless that word
echoes, so to speak, in the linguistic experience of
its audience, unless it "rings a bell" its meaning
remains stillborn, lifeless, a grunt or a growl. No
word stands alone. Every word is rooted in a articulated surround of meaning, a language and a culture.
There is no text without context. This context consists of all the horizons of the word's intelligibility, the finite bounds which "de-fine" or delimit
the word: not only the oral and written tradition,
i.e., everything that has explicitly been said and
done up to now, but also the unspoken myth, i.e.,
everything that "goes without saying" in a given language and culture and, not least, the spirit of the
whole discourse, i.e., everything that must needs
remain "unspeakable" in order to function as the common ground of understanding. Unless we share this
context to some extent, the Man speaking says nothing
(to us). His word is noise. To make sense of even
the simplest text, we must have some intelligence
concerning the entire cultural texture, its basic
principles and metaphysical assumptions -- what the
verb "to be" means, for instance, how time is exper-
ienced and its "tense" expressed, and so on -- we must
be in touch with the ultimate frontiers within which
people and peoples orient themselves, discover meaning
and live out their lives. To know the part (the
word), we must have at least an inkling of the whole
(not only the language, but the entire world it defines). In a word, there is constitutively a religious dimension to language: a bottomlessness, a dimension of more... than meets the eye or resounds in
the ear. Put another way, language without religion
is dead. It does not exist.

A Man hurls himself toward the Ultimate: He may leap into the air or stand stock still, he may kneel or prostrate himself, he may eat or he may fast, he may stay in our midst or else vanish from our sight on a spiritual quest whose aim and motivation may very well remain forever obscure to us. Why? What does he think he's doing? Where the devil is he going? On the phenomenological face of it, we know next to nothing about our neighbor's religious orientation. Whatever this Ultimate may mean to the Man, it is totally opaque to the rest of us unless he leave us some clue, a trace, a dance-step, perhaps, a map or a picture of his ecstatic itinerary, a tale told round the fire one dark night, a song sung in trance, an icon carved in wood or in stone... a simple word to mark his passing. To understand human life in its ultimacy, i.e., to bring its mystery at least somewhat within the bounds of our comprehension, we need words, or rites, or shared cultural patterns of meaning... if only to say that these words, etc., cannot "catch" that ineffable mystery. Religion without language (in all its cultural, artistic and cultic forms) remains vacuous, empty and, in the final analysis, unthinkable. Language, however, presents its own imponderables, especially when it comes to understanding one another's ultimate convictions. With 4-5,000 distinct languages jabbering all at once on our small planet, with complex congeries of dialect, idiolect, professional jargons and nomenclatures of all sorts within even a single language -- not to mention the thousand and one varieties of prevarication -- the entire linguistic universe would seem perversely calculated to increase only misunderstanding. Is it not amazing, given the odds against it, that we do occasionally manage to make sense to one another?! And yet it is precisely through this quite inscrutable "mystery of intelligibility" (language) that the irreducible dimension of mystery in all human affairs (religion) is rendered, to whatever degree, intelligible to us. Put another way, religion without language is incomprehensible.

On this dimensional interface, then -- this razor's edge between mystery and intelligibility, silence and the word, mythos and logos -- we begin to discern the bare outlines of the hybrid discipline of Religion and Literature. Admittedly, it is something of an orphan discipline these days: born some 20-odd years ago out of alienation and despair(2), abandoned early by its parent disciplines, weaned on paradox and contradiction(3), notorious for breaking the old school rules and now, like many another delinquent, panhandling in the academic marketplace with no visible means of support. At the very least, it has been a transient and truant studium all too often guilty of vagrancy, of uncritical and abortive attempts to study one discipline with methods proper to another. Examples abound: genre criticism and positivistic "analyses" of religious texts(4) or, the other way round, flat reductionism of great literature to (only) its ostensibly Christian themes.(5)

Of course interdisciplinary study, in Religion and Literature or anywhere else, does not mean just mixing up a saucy cocktail of methods; to each discipline, assuredly, belong its own methods. Nor, needless to say, can we settle for superficial dabbling and eclecticism, which does not "compare and contrast" very favorably with genuine scholarship. Is there no rigor here? Are we unable to envision the particular discipline(s) inherent to interdisciplinary studies? We had better hope we can do so... there are today, crowding in upon academia from all sides, fundamental issues -- social, environmental, personal -- issues of great moment which simply do not fit into the strictures of any single academic discipline. If we are to come thoughtfully to grips with such issues -- of God and Man, of Life, Death and everything in between -- we must find ways to study them in the light of the total human heritage of meaning and value. In this regard, I am willing to go out on a limb and humbly suggest that reading and writing may very well be the interdisciplinary disciplines par excellence, and quite possibly the least understood of our portals to the entire range of human experience. Reading and writing (that is to say, the more permanent forms of listening and talking) are so very basic that we tend to take them utterly for granted and ignore the crucial interpretive role they must play in any study of any issue whatsoever.

The quandary built into interdisciplinary studies altogether is a hermeneutical one, that is, a question of inter-pretation, of "going between" distinct universes of discourse without sacrificing coherence. When the interdisciplinary study in question is literature itself -- sacred and/or secular -- the quandary is redoubled, and the hermeneutic circle inescapable.(6) We have to use words (language) to talk about literature (language). Here, if anywhere, we must directly address the prejudices and presupposi-

xi

tions which affect and so often afflict interpretation across formerly impregnable disciplinary, linguistic, cultural and religious boundaries. As George Steiner has forthrightly put the case: All understanding -- within a given language as well as between languages -- amounts to translation.(7) There are no "pure" facts, somehow factual "in themselves;" there are only interpreted facts, facts "for us."(8) It is this interpretive or hermeneutical character of every eventuality in human experience that has led H.-G. Gadamer to affirm, echoing by inversion the Christian tradition of the incarnate Logos: "Being that can be understood is language."(9)

These focal considerations place the often wayward discipline of Religion and Literature in rather a special light. Gunn and Miller have each ably demonstrated from different angles(10) that many of the approaches which have unfortunately characterized research in this area over the past two decades have been both partial and parochial, although not without merit if properly conjoined to other such approaches. Religious texts have been treated as purely "literary" material (e.g., "The Bible as Literature"), while the works of unabashedly secular authors have been so to speak "mined" for their religious motifs (e.g., "Christianity in 19th Century American Fiction"). Another equally narrow approach, stemming either from a maladapted structuralism or the so-called New Criticism, has been to treat literature of any kind as a closed system of signs which are supposed to be decipherable within the linguistic world of the work itself, without reference to any larger cultural context. The shortcomings of such methodologies have long been apparent, but viable alternatives have been slow to surface.(11) Breakthroughs in method would seem to hinge on the two-fold observation made earlier: Religion has a constitutive linguistic dimension -- of logos, word, scripture, commentary and even scholasticism, not to mention icon, music, drama and the like. And, by the same token, no literature exists without roots and branches which shade off into certain undeniably ultimate horizons -- of mythos, ritual, prayer and mystery, not to mention cultural and personal assumptions, aspirations, and the like. Neither the word nor the spirit can survive apart from one another; isolated, were this even possible, the word could be no more than "dead letter" and the spirit sheer vacuity.

Now each religious tradition plainly has its own
attitudes toward the Word. Vāc in the śruti is not
identical to the Logos of the New Testament, although
there are striking similarities, and both clearly
differ from the cheng ming of the Confucian classics.
Moreover, each work of literature -- whether a religious classic or last week's bestseller -- is constructed in terms of its own ultimate concerns, which may
or may not be congruent with the priorities at issue
in another work. These things should be obvious.

But consider the implications for Religion and
Literature: The classical scriptures of the world's
religious traditions (even many of the oral traditions) today exist in modern languages, but they exist
mainly as literary artifacts, translations and adapta-
tions more or less stripped of the cultural (and
usually cultic) context in which they originally flourished, and often in dire need of critical appraisal in
terms of that context. So it is hardly farfetched to
suggest here that all the classics of world literature, most of which can properly be called religious
texts in their native milieux, today fall directly
within the purview of studies in Religion and Literature. Taken from the other angle, the same complex of
issues comes to light in the works of modern secular
authors who have long and deeply been exposed to this
global encounter of traditional worldviews. The literature of the 20th Century is saturated with motifs
arising not from a single language or tradition, but
from the wide world of millennial human experience in
all its rich and often perplexing diversity. In
order to understand many a contemporary writer, today's readers and critics find they must steep themselves in everything from the Vedas to the Eddas, from
medieval apocalyptic to amerindian creation stories.
What we read and the ways we read have been mutating
apace; it is a period of dizzying upheaval and unpredictable transformation. We find ourselves, willy-
nilly, in the midst of trying to assimilate the literatures of the global human community, and the plain
fact is that we do not entirely know how to go about
it, i.e., how to make sense across all these formidable barriers of space, time and culture. A glance at
the current state of international "relations" in the
global political and military arena ought to be sufficient confirmation as to how far out of hand the
problem has indeed gotten.

It is here, and for readers of English especially, that the difficult case of the poet Ezra Pound
becomes pivotal; the multi-lingual and multi-cultural
world of his Cantos confronts us with all the critical
dilemmas outlined above, and then some. Until the
present study, there has been remarkably little serious inquiry into the specifically cross-cultural and
religious issues raised by Pound and his work, perhaps
because Pound himself relished playing the role of
"the great pagan" and Religion and Literature as a
discipline has largely contented itself with books by
Christian authors for Christian audiences about Christian concerns. (T.S. Eliot's tiny corpus of poetry
has, for illustrious example, inspired a small library
of attempts to turn subtly-nuanced ambivalence into
straightforward Christian orthodoxy.(12)) The time
has come for a thoroughgoing reappraisal of the life
and works of Ezra Pound from the viewpoint of cross-
cultural religious studies. No other poet writing in
English in this century has so boldly set out "to
write an epic poem which begins 'in the Dark Forest,'
crosses the Purgatory of human error and ends in the
light."(13) Although the multi-cultural contours of
Pound's work do not always coincide with our more
comfortable judaeo-christian frames of reference, this
work does demonstrably draw from sources that can only
be called religious. One major concern of the present
book is to trace Pound's relations and rapports with
works he considered classics of the human spirit -- in
particular, those of Homer, Dante and Confucius. To
understand how Pound assimilates these diverse traditions, it is equally important to make explicit the
poet's self-understanding of his role as shaman --
visionary, traveler between worlds, self-healed healer,
guide of souls -- the mysterious figure who more than
likely represents the primordial homo religiosus in
the History of Religions.(14)

It is not our business, therefore, to elaborate
an a priori conceptual methodology -- with a known way,
it is said, one can only proceed to a known goal --,
but rather to examine close at hand Pound's own very
effective "ideogrammatic" method for allowing diverse
cultural, religious and linguistic matrices to meet
and fuse intelligibly in his work. In a manner of
speaking, this process involves the creation of a
multidimensional "sacred space," where the strangest
things become commonplace, and also vice-versa. Now a
method that works is comparable to long underwear in
winter: it is neatly tucked into its task, it does not

xiv

call attention to itself. Indeed, the more perfectly a method performs its function, the more readily it tends to disappear into that function and escape our notice. In order, then, to render visible Ezra Pound's methods for achieving this cross-cultural fusion -- as well as to gauge when he fails to do so -- we shall have to dive beneath the surface of what is said, and try to fathom why it is said and what exactly the poet conceives himself to be doing and saying. With Pound, this is not always easy.

When a poet in the middle of the 20th Century declares he has set out "to write Paradise," as Pound once described his project, several immediate difficulties confront the modern reader. What, for example, can he possibly mean by Paradise? Obviously, such a question must be addressed at the outset. And when this poet also happens to have been incarcerated in an insane asylum during 12 years of the composition of this putative "Paradiso" we are, to our shame, all too likely to shrug our critical shoulders and ignore both the poet and his poem -- even though such an enterprise, however well or poorly conceived, should by rights be of considerable interest to students and scholars of comparative literature, religion, philosophy and cultural anthropology. Certainly Pound's stature as a poet has by now been firmly established by Kenner, Davie, Pearlman and others. But despite this extensive and often brilliant existing Pound criticism, there remains a massive scholarly lacuna surrounding the relevance of Ezra Pound's work to disciplines other than English Literature. The following study can therefore be described as an exploratory attempt to interpret Pound's "Paradiso" in a coherent religious and philosophical light, thereby -- it is hoped -- clearing the way for this wider audience to enter "those high places, stirring and changeable"(15) of which The Cantos sing.

SE
Vernal Equinox, 1983
Catholic University of America

I The Walled Garden

1

"Life is, in itself and forever, shipwreck.
To be shipwrecked is not to drown. The poor human
being, feeling himself sinking into the abyss, moves
his arms to keep afloat. This movement of the arms
which is his reaction against his own destruction,
is culture -- a swimming stroke.-- When culture is
no more than this, it fulfills its function and the
human being rises above his own abyss. But ten
centuries of cultural continuity bring with it --
among many advantages -- the great disadvantage that
man believes himself safe, loses the feeling of
shipwreck, and his culture proceeds to burden itself
with parasitic and lymphatic matter. Some disconti-
nuity must therefore intervene, in order that man
may renew his feeling of peril, the substance of his
life. All his life-saving equipment must fail, he
must find nothing to cling to. Then his arms will
once again move redeemingly.
          "Consciousness of shipwreck, being the
truth of life, constitutes salvation. Hence I no
longer believe in any ideas except the ideas of
shipwrecked men. We must call the classics before a
court of shipwrecked men to answer certain peremp-
tory questions with reference to real life."

                          José Ortega y Gasset, 1932
                       "In Search of Goethe From Within"

1 The Myths of Paradise

> "It is difficult to write a
> paradiso when all the super-
> ficial indications are that
> you ought to write an
> apocalypse." (1)
>
> Ezra Pound

What meaning has "paradise" for modern man?

Very generally, it seems there is a restless-
ness, a discontent, an uneasiness (or even a "dis-
ease") built into the human condition. We are for
some reason never content with ourselves the way we
are. Our "position" in life never seems to us quite
satisfying or adequate or definitive. And so we
seek a better one.

From a purely formal and existential viewpoint,
William James, R. Panikkar and others have allowed
that all the phenomena we typically call religion
include: (A) a diagnosis of the given human situation, (B) the postulation of a "better place," and
(C) a prescription for getting from the one to the
other -- i.e., a religatio, a ligature, a bridge or
a link between here and there.(2) On this purely
formal level, regardless of whatever content one may
ascribe to its termini, religion may be definied as
the means employed to convey oneself from "A" to
"B".(3)

Therefore when the status of the "B" terminus
becomes questionable, this amounts to or may indeed
precipitate a religious crisis of the first magni-
tude. Today precisely this has occurred: Where are
we going? What is the meaning of "salvation" in the
post-Hiroshima world, a world in which planetary
human suicide has become a quite tangible danger?
One might call this startling state of affairs "no-
future shock." Indeed, once the ultimate frontier
of human life becomes questionable, what meaning has
the rest of it? How is it possible to "suffer" the
given human situation, "A", without hope of some
supernal respite from it, some "B"? Ours has been
called a "time of need."(4) Ours is the crucial
moment, the "hour of the wolf"(5), when the night is
dying and the new day as yet unborn. What is
happening to us? How did we lose our way?

3

First of all, Paradise (the "better place," the goal, the proper end of Man) is a myth.(6) In cultures where this tradition remains intact, the proper end of Man is taken quite for granted and thus presents a characteristically mythic structure. Myth here means a certain unquestioned backdrop over against which reality becomes meaningful, recognizable and, in point of fact, real: a context.(7) R. Panikkar has defined myth as an "horizon of intelligibility," that is, a certain orientation accepted as real by those who dwell within that horizon.(8)

For most of our forebears, the myth of the proper end of Man remained unquestionable and, hence, unquestioned. This is of course far from the case nowadays. Today the various "myths of paradise"(9) have encountered one another on a planetary scale, and have in a sense exposed one another as so many questionable presuppositions. As soon as one man, a Faust for example, refuses to enter the traditional paradise(10), the myth begins to break down. As soon as it can be questioned, the unquestionable ceases to exist as such. In Ezra Pound's words, "The dreams clash and are shattered." (11)

First to be discredited were our collective ideals: the otherworldly Heaven above, the so-called pie-in-the-sky, a future eternity which did nothing meanwhile to alleviate the suffering and indignity of this vale of tears here below; and next its this-worldly replacement, the secular Utopia hovering just over the horizon, an eternally futuristic future, so to speak, which never seemed to arrive either. Both capitalism and communism began as utopian ideals, but it has not gone unnoticed that "enlightened self-interest" has degenerated into a license for greed, or that the "dictatorship of the proletariat" has indefinitely postponed the true communist state. The massive geopolitical traumas of the 20th Century have left us equally cynical toward both the Heaven promised by revelation and the Perfect State promised by revolution. Instead, people have had little recourse but to take matters into their own hands and set up for themselves markedly individualistic goals on the empty horizon that once held out hope for the City of God or the City of Man. One well-known but extreme reaction is simply to cancel all bets on a collective human future and aim for some measure of worldly success, a real objective that can be gauged in

4

terms of profit, property or power. This option has
lately been undermined -- even in America, its native land -- not only by the economic collapse of
the materialistic "American Dream" but also by a
familiar internal inconsistency: the ruin of "the
inner man" just at the "peak" of his career. When
this happens, another extreme reaction to the loss
of paradise tends to set in, a narcissistic with-
drawal from "hard realities" into "states of mind,"
a search for what might be called the bliss that
will render one oblivious to any other goals. Now
altered states of consciousness are all very real
and often very useful, but the problem with supra-
normal states of mind as an ultimate is their fla-
grant transiency. There is always the morning
after...

   So it must be said that all of these "mirages"
of paradise today have failed us, or we have fallen
short of them. We are by and large indifferent to
the traditional collective eschatologies (sacred or
secular), which nowadays seem altogether incapable
of supporting the expectations with which they were
once invested. Nor have our modern individualistic
simulacra for these "lost" paradises fared any better, or disappointed us any less. Collectively and
individually, this far we have traveled. The broken
landmarks are all too familiar. But when our dreams
of paradise have all been shattered, where do we
turn? The perennial religious question reverberates
in the directionless void: Where do we go from
here? Even were we to proceed in much greater depth
and detail along the lines of the preceding sketch,
it is clear that we would find no plausible way out
of the impasse of human situation "A". The question
of the adequate "B" terminus of human life not only
remains distressingly unresolved, but seems to beg-
gar every effort to define it -- let alone attain
it.

"Be at home nowhere." (12)

Could it be that we have been peering through
the wrong end of our eschatological telescope? Perhaps we should not be asking how to get out of or
away from our proper reality, but how to enter it in
a new way. Let's look into this possibility.

The kinds of goals we were once able to content
ourselves with have generally exposed themselves as
escape routes, as it were "myths" of escape. Once
we diagnose our given situation as unsatisfactory --
for whatever reason -- we determine to leave it behind. Regrettably, it would seem that even in the
very formulation of our goals we take our given
limitations along as fellow travelers that will in
the end betray our loftiest dreams. The human predicament has become excruciating for modern or "ab-
surd" Man to the extent that he or she realizes
there is no way out of it.(13) Granting this dissolution and deterioration of the traditional "B"
termini, our human situation "A" today might well be
defined as precisely that situation from which there
is no escape. It is an exacerbated instance of the
hermeneutic circle(14): We cannot jump out of our
own skins. We cannot leave our proper reality behind without ceasing to be who we are.

Stanley Romaine Hopper once pointed out in this
context that the hermeneutic circle is a magic circle, an enchantment.(15) And you cannot break an
enchantment with a logical syllogism. What is
needed is a stronger enchantment, a new spell, a new
myth. And, as Schelling noted long ago, nobody can
invent a myth.(16) It emerges slowly, fitfully,
into logos. But new myths do appear in the passing
of obsolete ones (17), and archaic patterns reemerge
just where the veneer of "modernity" is wearing
thinnest. In our day, when the myths of paradise
all have broken down, Hopper underscores the awkward
truth that contemporary Man finds himself "thrust
radically upon the primary enigmas of existence."
In short, modern Man has been catapulted into the
primordial paradise of myth and stands -- utterly
dumbstruck and disoriented -- under a different
"star" ...a half-alien/half-familiar horizon: a new
myth.

The word paradise is often derived directly
from the Persian for "a walled garden." It is not a
garden to which there is no entrance, as we have
seen. Everybody has already staked out their own
little corner of the Elysian turf. No, it seems
rather that we have trapped ourselves within these
walls, and there is no exit. Out of frustration, or
exasperation, or just plain bewilderment, we begin
gingerly seeking to re-orient ourselves in this
garden of overgrown expectations. In the process,
it may happen that we get turned completely around
and suddenly find ourselves facing back-to-front.
We have attempted to escape with such singlemindedness
that we are quite unaccustomed to facing in
this direction. The insubstantial walls of mirage
against which we have vainly been dashing our collective and individual heads are now behind us.
They form only so many avenues of departure, and we
shall soon forget about them. Pound would say:
"What you depart from is not the way."(18) Ahead, a
strange and labyrinthine landscape beckons. We have
turned at long last toward the center, the point of
origin, the mysterious source. In whatever direction we happen to be facing, it will be at the
center that our paths inevitably cross.

This unknown at the center, this caelum incognitum to which we are now trepidatiously setting
forth, cannot be just an antithesis or a conceptual
counterpart to the "paradises" we have lost or
squandered up to now. We have no idea...which is as
it should be. The last thing humankind may need
today is another vision of the Promised Land. In
"not knowing" where we are going, i.e., in realizing
that we cannot get out of our proper realities, we
also acknowledge that we can only (in Heidegger's
phrase) "go toward where we already are"(19), and
perhaps (in Eliot's) come to "know the place for the
first time."(20)

If myth is that horizon of meaning within which
we always already find ourselves inscribed -- as it
were standing or falling -- then I would submit that
all our myths of paradise have metamorphosed into a
single though polyvalent myth of return.

Now to re-turn is never just to backtrack.
This much we have learned. We can neither go on in
the same direction nor go back. The re-turn is
another turning, another twist toward the center, a
re-sourcing as it were.(21) A myth is not an idea.

8

Myth is rather the substrate from which several, and
even sundry, ideational systems may grow.(22)   The
myth of return has been told in many tongues and
many ways down the ages. Homer tells of the sea
voyager attempting to navigate home. Dante tells of
the pilgrim's ascent toward the godhead.   In Ezra
Pound's work, these two horizons fuse.(23)   This
study is mainly an attempt to understand how such a
fusion is effected, and what it might mean.

Here it may be sufficient to point out that
myths of return and notions of afterlife are probably a good deal more ancient than human memory will
permit us to fathom. Nonetheless, some paradigms
have persisted with enough vitality to be considered
classic, i.e., perennially new. Homer's Odyssey is
one of the eldest(24), and certainly the most in-
fluential text where the myth of return is conjoined
with a vision of the afterlife.(25)

The 20th century has witnessed a remarkable
revival of interest -- to the point of preoccupation
-- in the Odyssey. From the authors and from the critical literature one gathers that in the limbo of
the Odyssey we may rediscover our own given human
situation ("A"), and -- if our luck holds -- gain
some inkling of the path, "wide as a hair"(26), up
from the underworld and into the light ("B").
Joyce's Ulysses(27) and Kazantzakis' The Odyssey, A
Modern Sequel(28) have captured more popular attention than Ezra Pound's Cantos, but it is on the
latter that we shall concentrate, for several very
specific reasons.

3 The Ultimate Odyssey

"A lost kind of experience?

                                        scarcely"(29)

   Patches of the Homeric fabric -- swatches of
pattern -- flare up periodically in Ezra Pound's poetic canon. Pound deals not only with Odysseus'
exploits at large or at random, but focuses preeminently on Book XI, the section of the original he
considered Homer's most archaic material: The
Nekuia, Odysseus' visit to the underworld. This
Hades -- an aimless, purposeless afterlife through
which wander the shades of the dead as if in a dream
-- strikes the modern reader as a state of affairs
not unlike our contemporary malaise d'esprit.(30)
Pound also saw it thus. He often juxtaposes to
current events Charon's question to Dante on the
river Styx: "You, in the dinghy astern there"(31);
what are you, a live man, doing here in the world of
the dead?

   The lineaments of the story are well known. In
Book XI, Odysseus, on Circe's instruction, must
descend to Hades and bid the blind seer Tiresias
(32) -- "Who even dead yet hath his mind entire"(33)
-- tell his doom over the blood of a black bell-
sheep. Odysseus' visit to the "other world" is in
fact the prerequisite of his return to Ithaca. It
is here he receives the token that will tell him
when he has completed his decade-long journey.(34)
It is here he is told, in Pound's minimal paraphrase: "Odysseus shalt return through spiteful
Neptune, over dark seas/ Lose all companions."
Pound will reiterate the journey again and again,
notably in Canto XLVII. One point stands out in
stark relief:

> This sound came in the dark
> First must thou go the road
>   to hell
> And to the bower of Ceres' daughter Proserpine,
> Through overhanging dark, to see Tiresias,
> Eyeless that was, a shade, that is in hell...
> Ere thou come to thy road's end.(35)

   The point that concerns us with regard to the
Odyssey re-emerging, and indeed redoubling its primordial power, in 20th century letters is not just
that it represents a return to the mythic stratum.

Rather, the Odyssey (and Dante's Commedia also, as we shall see) embodies certain dimensions of the myth of the return. Return is not just going back. There are certain prerequisites: "First must thou go the road to hell..." and one can never return quite the same way one came. Everything is put at hazard. In short, the myth of return presents a recognizably initiatory structure.

But initiation, rebirth; how does it apply? Odysseus is already an initiate before he goes down to Avernus. He has been born twice: once biologically a king, again socio-politically a victor in the trial-by-fire at Troy. The descent into the underworld is something else again, and precisely the theme on which Pound focuses his own odyssey: a third initiation, a further and deeper and wholly unexpected rupture of planes(36), a third and personal birth(37), into "higher" life, or "divine" life. In short, the focus is on apotheosis. In Canto 95, for example:

> That the wave crashed, whirling the raft, then
> Tearing the oar from his hand,
>   broke mast and yard-arm
> And he was drawn down under wave,
>   The wind tossing,
> Notus, Boreas,
>   as it were thistle-down.
> Then Leucothea had pity,
>   'mortal once
> Who is now a sea-god...' (38)

Or, as Pound repeatedly registers the Gods saying to one another of Odysseus: "With a mind like that, the man is one of us." But we must not get too far ahead of ourselves.

It will be our working hypothesis in what follows that Ezra Pound's "Paradiso" is above all his personal odyssey (a point about which there should be little dispute in critical circles), his attempted return to his own enigmatic Ithaca. Hence our intention here will be to map some of the contours of this ultimate odyssey. Keeping Odysseus in mind, we shall see that Pound always navigates by means of his craft(39), a term which should stand in all its ambiguity for Pound's poetic "method," or just his poetic. Our effort to understand Pound's craft will thus emphasize this "going between," the inter-pretive dimension to Pound's own work. In other words, it is

12

the perilous passage of the poet from "here" ("A") to
"there" ("B") which will mainly concern us hencefor-
ward.

   Meanwhile, we must abide for a time in limbo,
at least until we master the rudiments of the incan-
tation which will allow us to leave it behind. One
must carefully attend the lesser mysteries to attain
the greater, as did Odysseus in Pound's Canto I:

And then went down to the ship,
Set keel to breakers, forth on the godly sea...
            came we then to the place
Aforesaid by Circe.(40)
Here did they rites, Perimedes and Eurylochus,(41)
And drawing sword from my hip
I dug the ell-square pitkin;
Poured we libations unto each the dead,
First mead and then sweet wine, water mixed
                        with white flour.
Then prayed I many a prayer to the sickly
                        death's heads;
As set in Ithaca, sterile bulls of the best
For sacrifice, heaping the pyre with goods,
A sheep to Tiresias(42) only, black and a bell-sheep.
Dark blood flowed in the fosse,
Souls out of Erebus(43), cadaverous dead, of brides
Of youths and of the old who had borne much;
Souls stained with recent tears, girls tender,
Men many, mauled with bronze lance heads,
Battle spoil, bearing yet dreory arms,
These many crowded about me; with shouting,
Pallor upon me, cried to my men for more beasts;
Slaughtered the herds, sheep slain of bronze;
Poured ointment, cried to the gods,
To Pluto(44) the strong, and praised Proserpine;(45)
Unsheathed the narrow sword,
I sat to keep off the impetuous impotent dead,
Till I should hear Tiresias.
But first Elpenor came, our friend Elpenor...(46)
And Anticlea came(47), whom I beat off,
                  and then Tiresias Theban,
Holding his golden wand, knew me, and spoke first:
'A second time? why? man of ill star,
'Facing the sunless dead and this joyless region?
'Stand from the fosse, leave me my bloody bever
'For soothsay.'
          And I stepped back,
And he strong with the blood, said then: 'Odysseus
'Shalt return through spiteful Neptune, over dark seas,
'Lose all companions.'(48)

II <u>The Word As Image</u>*

"Energy creates pattern." (1)

Resonances between human language and the articulated rhythms, patterns and dynamisms of the natural world have long enraptured poets and philosophers alike; Man ever seeks to "read" the living text that is this Cosmos.

The tradition in American literature can be traced directly to Emerson, who wrote: "Things admit of being used as symbols because Nature is a symbol, in the whole and in every part."(2) Pound and his colleagues in the early 20th century not only inherited this tradition, but enriched it immensely: "The natural object is always the adequate symbol."(3) Curiously, this development in American letters parallels a similar turnabout in contemporary European philosophy, heralded by Husserl's famous injunction to return "to the things themselves."

The next three chapters examine some of the relations between certain patterns of metamorphosis in the natural world and certain verbal transformations in Ezra Pound's poetry. Thus the metaphor, presented here as the taproot of language and poetry, comes to flower in the Image of Pound's early poetry and critical essays, and in so doing discloses a depth dimension, a Vortex of sheer relativity between Heaven, Earth and Man. Moreover, Pound's attempt to articulate his own precarious rite of passage from Earth to Heaven brings to the fore the poet's role as shaman, mediator of the ongoing sacred marriage of Heaven and Earth.

In short, when things "speak for themselves," they tell us of one another.

*   *   *

I Metaphor

> I stood still and was a tree amid the wood,
> Knowing the truth of things unseen before;
> Of Daphne and the laurel bough,
> And that god-feasting couple old
> That grew elm-oak amid the wold.
> 'Twas not until the gods had been
> Kindly entreated, and been brought within
> Unto the hearth of their heart's home,
> That they might do this wonder thing;
> Nathless I have been a tree amid the wood
> And many a new thing understood
> That was rank folly to my head before. (4)

Ezra Pound chose 'The Tree' to stand for perpetuity as his first poem, first in the Pound canon. He obviously wanted us to begin from this beginning. And here, observe, already: an uncanny, extraordinarily precise attention to the Between, to the metaphorical threshold where there is commerce between dimensions of the real.

"I have been a tree amid the wood." Yes? How are we to fathom such a bold metaphor? The motif of metamorphosis is a persistent, almost dominant, chord in Pound's work, here drawn conspicuously from Ovid.(5) It is a thematic Pound strikes not only in his choice of subjects, but above all in his curious technique of paratactically juxtaposing topics, his lightning transits from one subject to another. Things turn into other things, people -- poets especially -- turn into other people, and then return to themselves. As Hugh Kenner and others have pointed out, metamorphosis -- pattern persisting through change -- is the skeleton key to the artistic unity of much of Pound's work.(6)

Going a step further, we may discern here a profound intuition into the metaphorical structure of language. Pound's preoccupation with the metaphor anticipates much European speculation on the same question by half a century.(7) A few years after penning 'The Tree,' we find Pound editing Ernest Fenollosa's short but seminal essay The Chinese Written Character As a Medium for Poetry(8), and there we read the following compact argument:

19

The whole delicate substance of speech is built upon substrata of metaphor. Abstract terms, pressed by etymology, reveal their ancient roots still embedded in direct action. But the primitive metaphors do not spring from arbitrary subjective processes. They are possible only because they follow objective lines of relation in nature herself. Relations are more real, and more important, than the things which they relate. The forces which produce the branch-angles of an oak lay potent in the acorn. Similar lines of resistance, half-curbing the outpressing vitalities, govern the branching of rivers and of nations. Thus a nerve, a wire, a roadway and a clearing house are only varying channels which communication forces for itself. This is more than an analogy. It is identity of structure. Nature furnishes her own clues. Had the world not been full of homologies, sympathies and identities, thought would have been starved and language chained to the obvious. There would have been no bridge whereby to cross from the minor truth of the seen to the major truth of the unseen.(9)

In this finely-wrought little essay, Fenollosa/Pound defines metaphor as "the use of material images to suggest immaterial relations." Precisely this process is our concern. The Fenollosa material can be considered a sort of poetic manifesto:

Metaphor, the revealer of nature, is the very substance of poetry. The known interprets the obscure, the universe is alive with myth. The beauty and freedom of the observed world furnish a model, and life is pregnant with art. The chief work of literary men, and of poets especially, lies in feeling back along the ancient lines of advance. The original metaphors stand as a kind of luminous background, giving color and vitality, forcing the words closer to the concreteness of natural processes.(10)

Here we have in statu nascendi the warp and the weft of the fabric Pound was to spend his life weaving in his verse. First, the focus on relationship, above all linguistic relativity: metaphor.(11) From this will emerge Pound's overarching rationale for his "ideogrammatic method"(12) of exhibiting on a single page "luminous details"(13) from disparate cultures, languages and poetic traditions. Secondly, from this concreteness of metaphor Pound will carry with him a life-long concern for "hyperscientific precision" in the use of words. This discloses the cosmological underpinnings of le mot juste(14) to be Fenollosa's "lines of relation in nature herself." And finally, we see already the interpretive thrust, the seeds of Pound's rigorous attention to the voices of tradition. It is also worthy of note that the whole enterprise is itself set into the metaphor of the return, the poet's odyssey unto origins. We can find in Fenollosa much of the thought that governs some of the most apparently arbitrary stylistic devices of The Cantos.

Earlier in the essay, Fenollosa had pointed out:

The sentence form was forced upon primitive men by nature itself. It was not we who made it, it was a reflection of the temporal order in causation. All truth has to be expressed in sentences because all truth is the transference of power. The type of sentence in nature is a flash of lightning. It passes between two terms; the cloud, and the earth. No unit of natural process can be less than this. All natural processes are, in their units, as much as this. Light, heat, gravity, chemical affinity, human will, have this in common: that they redistribute force. (15)

Once again, as we feel for our roots in the natural world, we find ourselves in the Between. The poet, the interpreter of the entire reality, is thus in so many words the one who goes between. It is this passage -- expressed eventually as sea voyage, or ascent into the celestial spheres -- this passage between worlds that will define for us, more than any other isolable invariant, Ezra Pound's poetic. Here also we begin to perceive the initiatory character of language as Pound conceives it: Every sentence is an initiation. Thus patterns of verbal manifestation reassemble under the magnetic sway of Pound's early vision into rites of passage. Later, in the churning ocean of The Cantos, it is in the proper performance of these rites(16) that the poet will find his only refuge and safety. Elsewhere we see him buffeted about mercilessly by waves and wind, hounded by the shades of the "impetuous impotent dead."(17)

21

It is a poetic which emphasizes the verb. The initiatory passage is verbal. Sentences are to rely on verbal tension, rather than on nominalist compression of substantives and modifiers. Fenollosa again, recommending that his reader examine the wealth of transitive verbs in Shakespeare:

> I have seldom seen our rhetoricians dwell on the fact that the great strength of our language lies in its splendid array of transitive verbs, drawn both from Anglo-Saxon and from Latin sources. They give us the most individual characterizations of force. Their power lies in their recognition of nature as a vast storehouse of forces. (18)

In ABC of Reading, Pound challenges the reader/ pupil to write a single page without using the verb to be.(19) It comes not easily; we have grown overfond of the convenient cupola. Fenollosa offers a path out of this bleak flatness. He bids us bear in mind that "Relations are more real, and more important, than the things which they relate... agent and object are but limiting terms."(20) We recall also Pound's insistence on translating an often-quoted line from Aristotle with the word "metaphor" where "relations" is the more conventional reading: "Swift perception of metaphor (relations), hallmark of genius." For Pound the emphasis must always be on energy, for "Energy creates pattern."(21) And the predominant verbal pattern is for him, as we have seen, the metaphor. But which metaphor? Which pattern? As soon as we ask the question, the contours of that primordial metaphor loom before us.

The "East" knew no Descartes. China and Japan knew no dichotomy between soul and body, subject and object. For Pound and some others, crossing the cultural threshold broke the back of the presiding occidental paradigms of intelligibility. Suddenly we are aswim in the "speculative" possibilities of language. Suddenly universality is not attainable by sweeping abstraction, but rather by careful attention and attunement to metaphorical "relativities." The direct fruit of Pound's encounter with Fenollosa's notes was the collection of nearly miraculous crib translations of Li Po (Rihaku) called Cathay, which won for Pound at least the opportunity to be dubbed by his friend Eliot "Inventor of China." Then came the Noh drama translations, somewhat less successful. And Pound's mature poetic only under-

22

scores his debt to Fenollosa; his fascination with China accompanied him to the end of his life.

We enter in The Chinese Written Character a linguistic world where it is quite reasonable to speak, as Pound often did, of an ideogrammatic method for writing poetry in English. At the very end of his disquisition, Fenollosa reflects on the possibilities and impossibilities of translating Chinese into English. He concludes:

> If we attempt to follow it in English, we must use words highly charged, words whose vital sugggestion shall interplay as nature interplays. Sentences must be like the mingling of the fringes of feathered banners, or as the colours of many flowers blended into the single sheen of a meadow.(22)

I should say that here lies the germ of the "pattern" Pound's Cantos will take, as the branch-angles of the oak lie potent in the acorn. We shall return to considerations of the Chinese language and Chinese context in Chapters 4-6.(23)

* * *

In his penetrating essay 'Le Cri de Merlini,' Stanley Hopper has noted that "when Pound uses a straight metaphor, he manages to preserve the discreteness and independence of the terms in the comparison."(24) This discipline persists throughout Pound's career. He enforces the tension between "relata" by focusing each term discretely, thus generating as it were a larger "gap" across which the spark of understanding must leap. He requires his readers to interpret him much as he himself would read the components of an ideogram: by taking everything into account. In his own eyes, he asks of his reader no more than he requires of himself.

In Pound's essay 'Psychology and Troubadors,' published in 1912 in G.R.S. Mead's The Quest and added to The Spirit of Romance, we should note the following unequivocal statement:

> An art is vital only so long as it is interpretive, so long that is that it manifests something which the artist perceives at greater

23

intensity and more intimately than his public. If he be the seeing man among the sightless, they will attend him only so long as his statements seem, or are proven, true. If he forsake this honor of interpreting, if he speak for the pleasure of hearing his own voice, they may listen for a little while to the babble and the sound of the painted words, but there comes, after a little, a murmur, a slight stirring, and then that condition which we see about us, disapproved as the "divorce of art and life."

The interpretive function is the highest honor of the arts, and because it is so we find that a sort of hyperscientific precision is the touchstone and assay of the artist's power, of his honor, his authenticity. Constantly, he must distinguish between the shades and the degrees of the ineffable. (25)

Pound's reflections on metaphor thus open out quite naturally onto the broader canvas of the arts in general, and poetry in particular. It is their interpretive character on which he concentrates. He will say later in the same essay:

The consciousness of some seems to rest, or to have its center more properly in what the Greek psychologists called the phantastikon. Their minds are, that is, circumvolved about them like soap bubbles, reflecting sundry patches of the macrocosmos. And with certain others, their consciousness is "germinal." Their thoughts are in them as the thought of the tree is in the seed, or in the grass, or the grain, or the blossom. And these minds are the more poetic, and they affect mind about them, and transmute it as the seed the earth. And this latter sort of mind is close on the vital universe, and the strength of the Greek beauty rests in this, that it is ever at the interpretation of this vital universe, by its signs of gods, godly attendants and oreads. (26)

There is probably no need to underscore this by employing a more technical hermeneutic vocabulary. Pound has done everything but invoke Hermes -- god of pilgrims and poets alike -- by name. It is enough to lament with Pound, in his Cavalcanti essay, that such matters are no longer transparent to us:

We appear to have lost the radiant world where one thought cuts through another with clean edge, a world of moving energies... magnetisms that take form, that are seen or that border on the visible, the matter of Dante's Paradiso, the glass under water, the form seen that seems a form seen in a mirror... (27)

"Energy creates pattern -- " The more carefully we read Pound, the more aware we become of the "shape" of this pattern. Natural processes have shape, a forma which as it were "in-forms" them, forms them from the inside out, the "god inside the stone"(28), "magnetisms that... border on the visible." There is a "shape" to The Cantos, as there is increasingly a "shape" to Pound's thought: "he observes a design in the Process"(29). A certain image recurs with almost hypnotic regularity and intensity:

For the modern scientist, energy has no borders, it is a shapeless "mass" of force; even his capacity to differentiate it to a degree never dreamed by the ancients has not led him to think of its shape or even its loci. The rose that his magnet makes in the iron filings does not lead him to think of the force in botanic terms or wish to visualize that force as floral and extant (ex-stare). (30)

From Pound's early attention to the metaphor, two branching paths may be discerned immediately. The one leads forward from what he subsequently called the "stale cream-puffs" of his A Lume Spento (31) and into the Imagisme we shall consider shortly. The other path deflects from the metaphor into his myriad translations, and to some extent accounts for his very personal appropriation of what he understood as "the tradition." In this context there is also the extraordinary phenomenon of Pound's personae. The figures who speak through many a Pound poem -- e.g. Bertran de Born(32), Acoetes(33), Philostratus(34), Kung(35), even Odysseus himself(36) -- are neither quite the original nor Pound's own, often cantankerous, "yatter." The personae are travelers, pilgrims moving toward a certain intelligibility, moving through an "open" poem, a reality itself unfinished, a "multiverse" still in the making, itinerant, on the move... (37) They attest a dynamism that is neither solely Pound's nor that of his many interlocutors.

One clue to Pound's work in translation, perhaps the unique contribution he has made here, is
his insistence on what can only be called the
revelatory character of truth. I mean to say that his
much-maligned "poetic license" is not a shortcoming at
all; it ought rather to be considered the saving grace
of his translations. Truth for Pound is not the
classical "correctness," although accuracy is an important element. But "fidelity" to a text, literal-
ness and so forth, can only be culturally bound,
temporally bound and linguistically bound. Something
must leap the gap, must "make it new"(38). Tradu-
tore/tradittore. Pound in his own way generates a
quite revolutionary reflection on the nature of truth,
strikingly congruent (as Stanley Hopper has shown)
with the "revealing and concealing" nature of aletheia
as Martin Heidegger understands that term.(39) For
Pound a translation rings "true" if it reveals the
intent of the original. He told his daughter, Marie
de Rachewiltz, when she set out to translate The
Cantos into Italian, "Don't translate what I said,
translate what I meant to say."(40)

The result is a new creation, a new poem. The
original is in a sense "concealed" in this new creation, in its contemporary revelation; concealed at
the same time and in the same words that it is
revealed. Pound never pretended to be a literal
translator. He translates as it were metaphori-
cally. If you set his translations side-by-side
with the orginal, Pound's work generally improves by
the contrast. His best translations bear a pecular,
diaphanous character. It is almost uncanny. Stanley Hopper has remarked in reference to Pound that
the "diaphanous"(41) -- a "showing through" -- and a
category Pound himself picked up while translating
Cavalcanti's canzone Donna Me Preigha(42) -- is by
far a more apt term for the revealing/concealing
character of truth than the Joycean epiphany (a
"showing upon")(43), a figure which has become somewhat shopworn in English and American literary critical circles over the past half century. We shall
eventually discover that Pound's "Paradiso" is also
arrayed in this "diaphanous" transparency, which is
not at all the failure to communicate it has so
often been construed.(44) Such a poetic, already
verging on a metaphysic of light, can and often does
culminate in verse of exquisite limpidity.

Not only in order to clarify Pound's mature poetic, but equally to point out some of the pitfalls likely to beset the modern reader in navigating through the later Cantos, we had best backtrack to about 1912. It is here that the "diaphanous" character of Pound's best verse first becomes apparent. Pound called what he was doing at the time Imagisme. In the following chapter, we shall examine a typical Imagiste artifact as if we had never seen one before.

Early in June 1913, some 18 months after a peculiar experience, Ezra Pound produced a small poem, as follows:

IN A STATION OF THE METRO

The apparition of these faces in the crowd;
Petals on a wet, black bough. (1)

At least we are often enough assured this is a poem. Poems, after all, are what poets make, and Mr. Untermeyer has included it in his 20th century English/American anthology of them.(2) Need we demand further criteria?

But of course. We find this is a famous poem, perhaps the "Imagiste"(3) poem par excellence, with reams of commentary to recommend it. Pound's own account of its gestation remains the most interesting, but Hugh Kenner's remarks add new information.(4) He tells us Pound made first "a 30 line poem, and destroyed it; after six months he wrote a shorter poem, also destroyed;" and after another year the one that he published. Here is Pound in T.P.'s Weekly, 6 June 1913:

> For well over a year, I have been trying to make a poem out of a very beautiful thing that befell me in the Paris underground. I got out of a train, at I think La Concorde, and in the jostle I saw a beautiful face, and then, turning suddenly, another, and then a beautiful child's face, and then another beautiful face. All that day I tried to find words for what this made me feel. That night, as I went home along the Rue Raynouard, I was still trying. I could get nothing but spots of color. I remember thinking that if I had been a painter, I might have started a whole new school of painting. I tried to write the poem weeks afterwards, in Italy, but found it useless. Then, only the other night, wondering how I should tell the adventure, it struck me that in Japan, where a work of art is not estimated by its acreage, and where sixteen syllables are accounted enough for a poem if you arrange and punctuate them properly, one might make a very

little poem, which would be translated about as follows:

"The apparition of these faces in the crowd;
Petals on a wet, black bough."

And there, or in some other very old, very quiet civilization, someone else might understand the significance."(5)

All right, this helps a great deal. But beyond what it seems to mean to Pound -- the resolution of an aesthetic impasse -- we encounter a paucity of critical criteria. What does it mean? What indeed is a poem? These are muddy waters; we are loathe to wet our feet. We hedge. We ask the author, then, "What is an image?", but Pound's immediate response -- "An Image is that which presents an intellectual and emotional complex in an instant of time."(6) -- leaves us at least as boggled as ever. We are however beginning to see the rather vast parameters of the puzzle this little poem poses.

What, then, does this particular poem refer to? What is signified?

Well, a Paris Metro station. The underground.

Let us go to the place.(7)

*   *   *

If one were not Ezra Pound, one might make a great deal of Impressionist fuss about the entrance to a Paris Metro. One walks from bright light, often enough, into a black maw spewing people. They emerge ashen, harried, stricken, to be suddenly washed with color by the sunlight exploring every mole, every pimple. Too much color. They blink past one another. Their faces are raw, excoriated, and they move much too rapidly, so that the colors blend and are lost in that movement. Enough to turn a strong stomach. Our poem is not here.

For Pound does not so fuss. He says: "The apparition of these faces in the crowd." By now we have passed the turnstile, yet met no apparition. The faces of the entering and exiting crowd are perhaps too real. They blot each other out, they

30

fall away. They do not quite appear; certainly not
with the sudden, discrete clarity of Pound's prose
account.

And inside? Lines. We have entered the
machine. Queuing to the right and to the left;
tunnels, tickets, destinations. Automata here render service to cash registers, gates open and close,
gears mesh, arrows point, bodies are moved. They
look... dead.

This is hell. It is perhaps, as Kenner
suggests(8), the ghastly lighting that turns the
faces to apparitions. Unsure, we drift with the
crowd into a nearby artery to the trains.

While so descending, we might reflect on our
passage, we might hear many subterranean echoes --
this girl, lost child, Koré(9) by the look of her;
and this big fellow with his eyes on her -- Dis?
Proserpine has dropped her flowers. And there,
Demeter running to reclaim her daughter for the
sunlit world?

But all these pictorial "images" are, well,
ludicrous in "this place where nothing grows."(10)
The infinite regress of white-tiled tunnels exhausts
their exuberance. And yet much exegetical effort
has been expended in this direction; analyzing,
categorizing, conceptualizing and generally pulling
asunder what the poet worked so hard to present
intact.

Despite the temptation to extrapolate, though,
is it not fairly obvious that Pound has put aside
the playthings of so-called "symbolist"(11) association? If the "referent" of the verse is the descent
into Hell, adumbraging Canto I, then Pound's little
poem is remarkable mainly for what it leaves out.
And can we say we have accounted for those "Petals
on a wet, black bough"? Perhaps we have merely been
catching at chimera -- leaves in maelstroms of our
own making, not leaves on a bough. All due deference to Hell, it seems insufficient exegesis for
these stubbornly precise two lines.

And so we come to the trains.

*   *   *

IN A STATION OF THE METRO

The apparition of these faces in the crowd;
Petals on a wet, black bough.

How curiously that semicolon juxtaposes these
two unlike lines! Conjoined and held apart in a
single stroke. The "apparition" is almost consumed
by track clatter; it registers an external landscape
with a rush, a bump and a jostle. But "Petals on a
wet, black bough," we can almost inhale. How differently it breathes; the thorny consonants and the
firm, deliberate comma nearly stop the voice to a
precise, polite puffing... a whisper, a sigh, a
rune, a cipher. A more private landscape -- perhaps
in the author's mind, perhaps internal to the poem
itself -- is subtlely but surely mapped out.

In Pound's Gaudier-Brzeska, A Memoir there is
another comment on this poem:

> I dare say it is meaningless unless one
> has drifted into a certain vein of thought. In
> a poem of this sort one is trying to record the
> precise instant when a thing outward and objec-
> tive [1st line] transforms itself, or darts
> into a thing inward and subjective [2nd line].
> (12)

Donald Davie, while commenting that here Pound
runs directly across the grain of les symbolistes,
also insists that "It is surely untrue.. that the
poem 'is meaningless unless one has drifted into a
certain vein of thought.' Its compactness is not
superficial, but real and masterly."(13) Nonetheless, a certain vein of thought does present itself
if we look at the poem in this way. The "outward/
inward" thrust of Pound's remark might lead us to
believe that the poet's "consciousness," whatever
that may be, is explicitly at issue here. Thus it
might lead us to suppose there might be some value
in applying "structuralist" techniques to the poem.
Let us examine this strategy.

We note that in Pound's Spirit of Romance,
published some years prior to his sojourn in the
Paris Metro, and reissued afterwards, he calls attention to the songs of the troubadors, notably
those of Arnaut Daniel(14), for introducing "explicitly a new lyric element... the matter of delay,
between the fine thing held in the mind and the

inferior thing ready for immediate consumption."(15)
Here we begin, in Hugh Kenner's fortunate phrase,
"to savor the contrast of the vegetal world with the
world of machines."(16) But now, do you see, we
have boarded the train...

'In A Station of the Metro,' we board a train
to all possible stations of the Metro. To master
the code, all systems of exchange and transformation
must be exposed along an intelligible armature.(17)
The total field of choices and decisions we have
before us, while still finite, expands radically.(18)

We may look in Pound's later work for homolo-
gues, with 50 years making a difference only in
refinement of style. The terms of the comparison --
the human world and the organic -- vary widely, but
the pattern of their juxtaposition remains ever
intact. Canto 106 is a far-flung instance:

> This Tzu could guide you in some things,
> but not hither,
> how to govern is from the time of Kuan Chung,
> but the cup of white gold at Patera,
> Helen's breasts gave that. (19)

Or we may choose to see a dipolar structure in
the falling/rising rhythm of the passage which com-
pletes another journey to and from the Underworld in
Canto XLVII:

> Hast'ou a deeper planting,
> doth thy death year
> bring swifter shoot?
> Hast'ou entered more deeply the mountain?
> . . .
>
> Splendour on splendour!
> By prong have I entered these hills:
> That the grass grow from my body,
> That I hear the roots speaking together,
> The air is new on my leaf,
> The forked boughs shake with the wind.
> . . .
>
> By this door have I entered the hill.
> Falleth,
> Adonis falleth.
> Fruit cometh after. (20)

And this is not all we may see in this vein.
The choice of Canto I as the beginning of Pound's
own poetic odyssey can be clarified. With an eye to
the "structure" of Odysseus' descent to the Underworld, we are better able to grasp Pound's description of The Cantos "main scheme" in a letter to his
father, Homer(I) Pound, dated 11 April 1927:

> Rather like, or unlike, subject and response
> and counter-subject in fugue:

>> AA Live man goes down into world of dead
>> CB The "repeat in history"
>> BC The "magic moment" or moment of meta-
>> morphosis, bust through from quotidian
>> into "divine or permanent world."
>> Gods, etc. (21)

This passage can be one very important clue to
the coherence of The Cantos.(22) But we must not
abuse it by taking it for more than it is. How easy
it would be to prop up a paradigmatic chain of
signifiers this way! Taking our leave from Levi-
Strauss and linking this and that by the smallest
difference between links, we might start with the
Metro poem as one of our key "poethemes." As we
have illustrated, it is possible to strike a rich
paradigmatic vein here. Even the last lines of
Pound's 'Tree,' which we considered briefly at the
outset, come into sharper focus:

> Nathless I have been a tree amid the wood,
> And many a new thing understood
> That was rank folly to my head before. (23)

Dr. Kenner apparently inspired some disbelief
in a 1972 lecture at Claremont College with his
suggestion that Pound went silent for several years
at the end of his long life ("silence seized me")
because he had always wanted to be a tree. This is
however a most appropriate observation, partly because it does not explain...

But now, with our galaxy of structurally inter-
dependent referential coordinates spread out all
around the tiny poem on which they seem to converge,
we find ourselves still at sea.

If we go on hunting for "structuralist" paradigms, we have to admit that one poem more or less
matters only slightly. Nearly all of our conceptual

operations can be performed without it. From a
structuralist perspective, it can be said that a man
writes a single poem all his days, and that it is
all its versions. We might multiply and divide
examples ad infinitum, but do we not lose something
incalculable amidst our calculations? Do we not
lose specifically our two-line poem under the hay-
stack of "poethemes" and so forth? We lose the
concreteness Pound so valued, the unique acuity of
each discrete perception. The "metalinguistic"
armature we would construct is so vast that it
becomes murky, squashy, unkempt. The individual
lines retain but positional value. They have become
mere counters. Calling them up/down, open/closed,
nature/culture or whatever, cannot in itself recoup
the loss.

Our first attempt, to represent the poem as
only the signified "underground" setting, gained us
a mushy fullness, congealed and shimmering, an irri-
descent bubble of pleromatic froth. This would make
Pound's work appear an indulgence, a gush of sentiment over a "better day" long gone, when the gods
walked with men, a "nostalgie de la boue" candied in
a nostalgia for paradise. Syrup. It would also
contain the presumption that the pictorial "image"
we happen to see is the same one that Pound himself
saw that day in the Metro.

Our second attempt, this time more "scientifi-
cally" to represent the poem as only the words on
the page, gained us a paradigmatic chain of signifiers and an ineradicable split, running from the
very earliest Pound poem to the end of his career
like a personal San Andreas fault. Carried to an
extreme, this method of exegesis would probably
leave Pound in the "looney bin."(24) It is all too
easy to make of Pound a "type," a sort of mad brico-
leur(25) darting hither and yon disguised as a gad-
fly impressario dangling oddments of his arcanum
from elbows and fingertips. A puppets-master, at
best. This is also to say that what we ourselves
see in his poem ever is and must remain different,
cut off, from what Pound saw that day in the Paris
underground.

What happens when cosmological identity meets
epistemological difference? "Shall two know the
same in their knowing?"(26)

35

Indeed, we are still lost. In the end it becomes evident that one may board all the trains to all the destinations marked neatly above all the tunnels, and never arrive at this particular little poem.

Once again, we are brought to a curious halt: "IN A STATION OF THE METRO." Perhaps our exertions have tired out the critical faculty. We may pull up a bench, indulge in some black tobacco, and muse here a while.

                    *   *   *

All the exegesis we have so far attempted seems fruitless in the face of the sui generis event with which the poem concerns itself. We begin to despair of ever finding the poem in this maze of preconceived interpretive options. All our cogitation seems but an affair of one- and two-way shuttles down a track constantly retreating into multiple vanishing points.

Perhaps it was all nonsense. Pound's "Image" could just be some sort of arbitrary intellectual construct anyway; to go hunting for it in the Paris mass transit system could only be the zenith (or the nadir) of foolish literalism. We squirm on the bench. We look up furtively. There is perhaps a pretty girl standing on the far platform, across the tracks.

The tunnel begins rumbling, heavy with train. Other people gather round, but... such a pretty face. We keep looking.

It doesn't really matter whether it is a pretty face that keeps one's attention (though it helps); only that we continue to look across the tracks when we would normally allow our eyes to be carried by the moving train.

A single train is best, and one either departing or not stopping at this station. And the effect is probably better if the train is closer to you than to her. Then a most astonishing thing occurs:

IN A STATION OF THE METRO

The apparition of these faces in the crowd;
Petals on a wet, black bough.

Impossible to describe this adequately. One
ends up listing qualities, properties, perspective,
substance, accident, illusion and the like. It
doesn't even quite jibe with Pound's prose account,
though the intervening 18 months might have stream-
lined the memory. But it happens. The poem suddenly "borders on the visible": The dark, rushing
train carriage forms the "branch," gold and white
lettering the "wet," and in each window our young
lady's face, and that of anyone else queuing up, has
been kaleidoscoped into a spinning crystal of
colors. Discrete, one flower-face -- or is it a
bud? -- appearing in the unforeseen "window" through
which one peers, as it were between the actual
windows which are passing rapidly as frames through
a motion picture projector. And the whole takes
place in what Pound might call a "phantom dawn"(27)
produced by the fluorescent lighting in the outer
station melding with the incandescent coach lights
inside the train. The effect is literally dazzling.

                    *   *   *

One way to approach Pound's achievement in this
tiny tour de force is to note that he has shifted
our understanding of image, and thus of imagination,
from the "view" still prevalent in western culture
of imagination as "picture thinking"(28) to a verbal
and linguistic basis. We are presented two such
conventional pictorial images: faces in a crowd,
petals on a bough. From our sojourn in the underground, we have learned that it is not these "pictures," but rather the dynamic of their interplay
(with one another and with us as well) which Pound
calls Image. It is here that Pound intersects and
to some extent anticipates the more recent work of
Heidegger, Paul Ricoeur, et al.(29)

We have found that all the possible "represen-
tations" of it simply do not exhaust the reality of
this little poem. In short, in order to juxtapose
the two pictorial images -- faces, petals -- you
have to use your imagination. The Image thus gener-
ated is not a static picture but a process, a "pattern persisting through changing circumstances."(30)

It is this little poem which inaugurates a shift (at least in English letters) from nouns to verbs, from "picture thinking" to "refinement of language"(31), from nominalism to dynamism. The metaphor and its verbal tension between relata becomes the criterion of intelligibility, replacing the Renaissance/Enlightenment XYZ perceptual grid, with its "perspective" and its "vanishing point."(32) Suddenly reality is no longer monochromatic or monotonous, but multidimensional and diaphanous.

Now slow down!, someone is likely to retort. There is in this Metro poem no verb at all. How can it attest a verbal basis for the imagination if the poem contains no verb?

This may well be the point. The poem "contains" no verb because this poem in its entirety IS a verb, i.e., it is wholly verbalized. In Fenollosa's terms, the entire Image functions as a "transference of power." Nothing could be more natural.

* * *

Between the two lines of this simple poem, a rift(33), a chasm, a whirlpool has opened out before us. Pound will soon come to call it vortex. In the magic moment of diaphany we seem to hover at the brink of some unfathomable mystery: "An image...is real because we know it directly."(34) Indeed! The Image itself turns out to be the event we so painstakingly sought in the Paris metro, not a facsimile thereof. The maelstrom of interpretive options follows from the inexhaustibility of any real thing. We could investigate its ramifications forever. In short, we have entered the Vortex.

"The Image is not an Idea. It
is a radiant node or cluster;
it is what I can, and must
perforce, call a VORTEX --
from which, and through which,
and into which, ideas are constantly rushing."(1)

The sculptor Henri Gaudier-Brzeska, before his
premature death in World War I(2), left the world
several small stone figures, numerous drawings, a
few letters of exceptional vitality and intensity,
and the essay Vortex, which begins: "Sculptural
energy is the mountain." Pound translated this
essay from its native French into English, probably
titled it, and is certainly responsible -- hand in
hand with the volcanic and indefatigable Wyndham
Lewis(3) -- for the name "Vorticism" coming into
vogue among the small coterie of artists who launch-
ed themselves under its banner before the Great War
(terminally) interrupted them.(4)

Gaudier's astounding little essay has been
presented by Pound, citing John Cournos' remarks to
this effect, as the first "world history of
sculpture." It is worth exhibiting in toto. (Exhibit follows this chapter.)

Meanwhile, Kenner summarizes it elegantly:

Thus, as John Cournos noticed, Gaudier's
"Vortex" was an idiosyncratic history of sculpture. Each civilization had its individuating
system of forms, the system, more profound than
"style," by which we know Egyptian work from
Assyrian. Gaudier postulated a metamorphosis
of characterizing sculptural forms: the sphere
drawn up into the Egyptian pyramid, pulled
lengthwise into the Oceanic cylinder, com-
pressed into Assyrian "splendid squatness," the
sculptural vortex in each place ingathering the
natural forms -- cats, phalli, bulls -- that
Greek decadence was content to measure and
copy. By formal allusion a 1914 sculptor could
draw on these resources of power; Gaudier's
"Hieratic Head of Ezra Pound" is Oceanic/Egyp-
tian. (5)

41

In Gaudier's eye, the presiding formal perceptions (square, conic, spherical, etc.) of major
cultural matrices -- Greek, Semitic, Hamitic, Chinese
African, Oceanic -- flow fluidly into and out of one
another, and permeate as well the whole cloth of a
given civilization. In calling down Ming decadence,
for example, Gaudier's geometry acquires ethical
overtones: "The sphere lost significance and they
admired themselves."

Gaudier's terse commentary reveals a "formal"
continuity, a balance between the diverse accultura-
tions of form, without failing to respect their
unique genii loci. It is a most curious document.
In a sense, Gaudier had mapped out the "shape" of
the "vector equilibrium"(6) long before R. Buckminster Fuller gave it an appropriate name. We shall
explore this geomancy more thoroughly in the Illustrations.

Gaudier concludes his essay with a summary of
what he considers his own "formal" situation:

The knowledge of our civilization embraces
the world, we have mastered the elements.
We have crystallized the sphere into the cube.
We have made a combination of all the possible
shaped masses.

It is not surprising that only a very few people
supposed they knew what Gaudier was talking about,
but Pound certainly considered himself chief among
the claimants. Beyond its propensity for transforming forms into other forms, Gaudier's planetary
"spectrum" of form value figures in Pound's later
work in another, obliquely powerful, way. It is in
Pound's famous "rock-drill action"(7), the uncompro-
mising thrust toward the very center of "the matter,"
that we can gauge Gaudier's impact on him.(8)   Accordingly, this center toward which Pound keeps
"hammering away" is less and less a "place" (or even
a concept), more and more this vortex, this "clearing"
of the center, a process it is fair to characterize
as a kenosis -- an emptying, or an opening.

Accompanying and reinforcing his attention to
Gaudier, we ought also to be aware of Pound's careful reading and review of two books by Allen Upward:
The Divine Mystery, and The New Word.(9) We shall
return to the former shortly.

42

I believe Donald Davie, in his recent Ezra
Pound(10), is the first to point out the passage in
Upward's New Word concerning the waterspout as a
"double vortex":

The story of the waterspout as it is told in
books shows it to be a brief-lived tree. A
cloud is whirling downwards and thrusting out
its whirlpoint to the sea, like a sucking mouth.
The sea below whirls upwards, thrusting out its
whirlpoint towards the cloud. The two ends
meet and the water swept up in the sea-whirl
passes on into the cloud-whirl, and swirls up
through it, as it were gainsaying it.

In the ideal waterspout, not only does the
water... swirl upwards through the cloud-swirl,
but the cloud swirls downwards through the sea-
swirl.

The ideal waterspout is not yet complete; the
upper half must unfold like a fan, only it
unfolds all around, like a flower-cup, and it
does not leave the cup empty, so that this
flower is like a chrysanthemum. And at the
same time the lower half has unfolded in the
same way, til there are two chrysanthemums back
to back...

It is Strength turning inside out. Such is the
true beat of Strength, the first beat, the one
from which all others part, the beat which we
feel in all things that come within our measure, in ourselves, and in our starry world.(11)

Davie comments: "Upward did not live to see
this inspired guess at 'the first beat' astonish-
ingly confirmed... when the biophysicists Crick and
Watson broke the genetic code to reveal the 'double
helix' (that is to say, double vortex)." (12) But
Pound did. And he also lived to meet Buckminster
Fuller (13), whose tetrahelix elegantly models its
principles. (14)

Upward's account qualifies to some degree as a
mystical vision. Whatever its value, it is a vision
Pound shared. Matter is a matter of perspective.
Before giving his waterspout image, Upward suggests
for matter the model of two wrestlers locked together, motionless. By this we are meant to understand so-called "solids" as a patterning of forces.

43

But the wrestlers are an inadequate model; as Davie
notes, they would have to turn into each other. (15)
The waterspout is the revealing image.

What we have been observing are patterns of
metamorphosis, the natural rites of passage. If the
only norm is change, its only constants are the
patterns through which things transform themselves
and one another: the patterns of growth. For Pound
metamorphosis is a constant; it is not simply a
transition from one status quo to another. The
change is radical -- ever changing -- and has more
the character of a standing wave, a fluxus quo. In
such a vision, the universe, the single song sung in
many tongues (aliter, The Cantos), is verbal and
syntropic, not nominal and entropic. The sentence
does not "mimic" nature, it is a natural "transference of power."(16) The living word (i.e., the new
word) embodies living "forces." It is not a copy of
anything.

The other Upward book swept into this central
current of Pound's work was The Divine Mystery,
disarmingly subtitled 'A Reading of the History of
Christianity Down to the Birth of Christ.' (17) In
this brilliant though idiosyncratic treatise, Upward
begins by discussing the Wizard, the Magician, the
Genius, the Seer, the Priest and the Prophet. All
are in his terms archetypes or prototypes of the
Christ to come. In modern-day History of Religions'
nomenclature, these are all figures for the Shaman,
"types" resulting from the disintegration of the
primordial Shaman into Prophet and Priest, mystic
and scientific wizard, etc. (18) The pattern is a
familiar one.

In Upward's hierarchy, this "Genius" first
comes to light as the Wizard, or Medicine Man -- and
also the Rainmaker with which Pound readers are
acquainted from the Frobenius context (19), whose
"antennae" are a little sharper than those of his
neighbors, so that he feels the storm or the rain
before its onset. It is difficult to convey the
impact of Upward's swift, sure style -- and thus a
good part of the effect if had on Pound -- without
quoting him just a little. Chapter 1.1, 'The Son of
Thunder,' begins magically:

I was sitting like Abraham in my tent door in
the heat of the day, outside a pagan city of
Africa, when the Lord of the Thunder appeared

44

before me, going on his way into the town to
call down thunder from heaven upon it.

He had on his Wizard's robe, hung round with
magical shells that rattled as he moved; and
there walked beside him a young man carrying a
lute. I gave the magician a piece of silver,
and he danced before me the dance that draws
down the thunder. After which he went his way
into the town; and the people were gathered
together in the courtyard of the king's house;
and he danced before them all. Then it thun-
dered for the first time in many days, and the
king gave the Thunder Maker a black goat -- the
immemorial reward of the performing god.

So begins the history of the Divine Man, and
such is his rude nativity. The secret of Genius is sensitiveness. The Genius of the Thunder who revealed himself to me could not call
the thunder, but he could be called by it. (20)

Thus Pound would come to speak of artists as
the "antennae of the race." It can be said that the
Rainmaker interprets Heaven to Earth. His is the
responsibility to make the one clear -- or cloudy, as
the case may be -- to the other. This translation of
Heaven to Earth has long been the model of the
poet's role. Consider Homer, Dante, Confucius.
Gather them together, as Pound did. You will begin
to see, again, "bordering on the visible," the dark
shade of the protean Shaman, whose mandate it is to
translate the heavens to those more terrestrial than
he, more subject to gravity...

This shaman/poet may most simply be described
as the traveler between worlds or, better said perhaps, between dimensions of the real... the heavenly, the earthly and the human realms. He is the
interpreter of the text that is this Cosmos. He is
the healer, the one who makes whole. And traditionally he is also the psychopomp, guide of souls.

Today, his traditional functions suspended in
the crush of materialism, the poet/shaman cannot but
be put in crisis. It is not that there are no
purely "primitive" cultures left. It is not even
that there is no room left in our own society for
anyone who does not "earn" their living (but rather
celebrates it, and thereby abets the renewal of all
life). No, it is rather that today the shaman psy-

45

chopompos seems to have no place to lead the souls.
There is nowhere left to run, let alone to dance out
the mysteries. All the splendid myths of paradise
seem to crumble just as they come within our reach.
The "modern" poet finds himself condemned to a flat
world, a prison house of two dimensions (or, in
Pound's case, an insane asylum). The great risk of
passing between worlds, as Odysseus discovered, is
that the return is always the more difficult leg of
the journey. One may as it were get "stuck" between
worlds, neither here nor there; as Odysseus did for
nine years on the island of the divine Calypso ("the
hidden"), and as Pound in his way did also, for 12
years of stark exile in the land of his birth.
During which period, be it noted, he composed those
Cantos generally considered to constitute his "Paradiso."

But again we are ahead of ourselves. It is
enough that we observe Pound's increasing reliance
on this crucial passage: between cultures, between
personae, between Earth and Heaven, between...
worlds. Three "worlds" emerge quite distinctly in
Pound's later work: keeping to our terminology(21),
they are the cosmological, the anthropological and
the theological. In Pound's Chinese vocabulary,
they are simply Earth, Man and Heaven.

To this point, we have examined the metaphor,
and seen it blossom into the image. We have plumbed
one such image deeply enough to recognize in its
subjective/objective commerce as it were an abyss, a
fissure, an opening, a vortex, a swirling fluxus
quo. And we have examined some of the features of
this cosmological locus. Now we shall begin a transition to the anthropological horizon of Pound's
work. This is easily done, since Pound effected
such a transition himself. In his Chinese translations, this "norm of change" is called the unwobbling pivot or, more rarely, the Great Balance. In
a nutshell, from Canto 99:

Heaven, man, earth, our law as written
        not outside their natural colour (22)

If Pound could see in Upward's "Genius" the
prototypical poet, he also knew very well the risks
of attempting to perpetrate such a persona in the
20th century. His Chinese studies gave him confidence -- perhaps too much confidence -- that the Great
Balance between the three worlds can be kept; in-

deed, can only be kept. Thus he dared, with the
publication of the first installment of Cantos, to
present the world with an open poem, an unfinished
magnum opus. At respectable intervals he himself
declared he had no idea how it would turn out. Or
he would drop asides about having it all "caught up
in music" at the end. Ultimately, he believed he
could not finish his poem. Others say it finished
him. We shall take up this discussion in Chapter 8.
But if we did not have The Cantos, the following
(and final) paragraph from Upward's Divine Mystery
might well have been an appropriate coda to the life
and times of one Ezra Pound, "man of ill star":

> If the foregoing pages point to any truth,
> it seems to be that the Divine Man is a type of
> the divine in man. The race is not promoted
> all at once, nor all together. The higher race
> comes at first in single spies, instead of in
> battalions. The prophet is thus, in the words
> of Paul, an abortion, born out of due time,
> dowered with the thoughts and feelings of the
> next generation rather than his own. He suf-
> fers accordingly, suffers in a world whose ways
> are strange to him, and in which his course
> among the Earthmen with whom his lot is cast
> may be compared to that of a dancer in the
> Orphic mysteries, brought by his progress into
> rude collision with the barbarian throng,
> treading their different measure in honour of
> their bloody Earth Gods. He suffers on behalf
> of mankind, since he is a pioneer, making the
> way smooth for all that are to follow. He is
> the gentleman of the future; he is the king of
> tomorrow, and the aureole of genius is his
> crown of thorns. (23)

As it were Hugh Selwyn Mauberley, his epitaph.
(24)

STAG (*in the* Chinese manner). 1913.
Pen and Indian Ink

VORTEX*

Gaudier-Brzeska

Sculptural energy is the mountain.

Sculptural feeling is the appreciation of masses in relation.

Sculptural ability is the defining of these masses by planes.

The paleolithic vortex resulted in the decoration of the Dordogne caverns.

Early stone-age man disputed the earth with animals.

His livelihood depended on the hazards of the hunt— his greatest victory the domestication of a few species.

Out of the minds primordially preoccupied with animals Fonts-de-Gaume gained its procession of horses

49

carved in the rock. The driving power was life in the absolute -- the plastic expression the fruitful sphere.

The sphere is thrown through space, it is the soul and object of the vortex --

The intensity of existence had revealed to man a truth of form -- his manhood was strained to the highest potential -- his energy brutal -- his opulent maturity was convex.

The acute fight subsided at the birth of the three primary civilizations. It always retained more intensity East.

The hamite vortex of Egypt, the land of plenty --

Man succeeded in his far reaching speculations -- Honour to the divinity!

Religion pushed him to the use of the vertical which inspires awe. His gods were self made, he built them in his image, and retained as much of the sphere as could round the sharpness of the parallelogram.

He preferred the pyramid to the mastaba.

The fair Greek felt this influence across the middle seas.

The fair Greek saw himself only. He petrified his own semblance.

His sculpture was derivative, his feeling for form secondary. The absence of direct energy lasted for a thousand years.

The Indians felt the hamitic influence through Greek spectacles. Their extreme temperament inclined towards asceticism, admiration of non-desire as a balance against abuse produced a kind of sculpture without new form perception -- and which is the result of the peculiar

VORTEX OF BLACKNESS AND SILENCE

Plastic soul is intensity of life bursting the plane.

The Germanic barbarians were verily whirled by the mysterious need of acquiring new arable lands. They moved restlessly, like strong oxen stampeding.

50

The semitic vortex was the lust of war. The men of Elam, of Assur, of Bebel and the Kheta, the men of Armenia and those of Canaan had to slay each other cruelly for the possession of fertile valleys. Their gods sent them the vertical direction, the earth, the sphere.

They elevated the sphere in a splendid squatness and created the horizontal.

From Sargon to Amir-nasir-pal men built manheaded bulls in horizontal flight-walk. Men flayed their captives alive and erected howling lions: the elongated horizontal sphere buttressed on four columns, and their kingdoms disappeared.

Christ flourished and perished in Yudah.

Christianity gained Africa, and from the seaports of the Mediterranean it won the Roman Empire.

The stampeding Franks came into violent contact with it as well as the Greco-Roman tradition.

They were swamped by the remote reflections of the two vortices of the West.

Gothic sculpture was but a faint echo of the hamito-semitic energies through Roman traditions, and it lasted half a thousand years, and it wilfully divagated again into the Greek derivation from the land of Amen-Ra.

Vortex of a Vortex!

Vortex is the point one and indivisible!

Vortex is energy! and it gave forth solid excrements in the quattro e cinque cento, liquid until the seventeenth century, gases whistle till now. This is the history of form value in the West until the fall of impressionism.

The black-haired men who wandered through the pass of Khotan into the Valley of the Yellow River lived peacefully tilling their lands, and they grew prosperous.

Their paleolithic feeling was intensified. As gods they had themselves in the persons of their human ancestors -- and of the spirits of the horse and of the land and the grain.

The sphere swayed.

51

The vortex was absolute.

The Shang and Chow dynasties produced the convex bronze vases.

The features of Tao-t'ie were inscribed inside of the square with the rounded corners -- the centuple spherical frog presided over the inverted truncated cone that is the bronze war drum.

The vortex was intense maturity. Maturity is fecundity -- they grew numerous and it lasted for six thousand years.

The force relapsed and they accumulated wealth, forsook their work, and after losing their form-understanding through the Han and T'ang dynasties, they founded the Ming and found artistic ruin and sterility.

The sphere lost significance and they admired themselves.

During their great period off-shoots from their race had landed on another continent. -- After many wanderings some tribes settled on the highlands of Yukatan and Mexico.

When the Ming were losing their conception, these neo-Mongols had a flourishing state. Through the strain of warfare they submitted the Chinese sphere to horizontal treatment much as the Semites had done. Their cruel nature and temperament supplied them with a stimulant: the vortex of destruction.

Besides these highly developed peoples there lived on the world other races inhabiting Africa and the Ocean islands.

When we first knew them they were very near the paleolithic stage. Though they were not so much dependent upon animals their expenditure of energy was wide, for they began to till the land and practice crafts rationally, and they fell into contemplation before their sex: the site of their great energy: their convex maturity.

They pulled the sphere lengthways and made the cylinder, this is the vortex of fecundity, and it has left us the masterpieces that are known as love charms.

52

The soil was hard, material difficult to win from nature, storms frequent, as also fevers and other epidemics. They got frightened: This is the vortex of fear, its mass is the pointed cone, its masterpieces the fetishes.

And we the moderns: Epstein, Brancusi, Archipenko, Dunikowski, Modigliani, and myself, through the incessant struggle in the complex city, have likewise to spend much energy.

The knowledge of our civilization embraces the world, we have mastered the elements.

We have been influenced by what we liked most, each according to his own individuality, we have crystallized the sphere into the cube, we have made a combination of all the possible shaped masses -- concentrating them to express our abstract thoughts of conscious superiority.

Will and consciousness are our

VORTEX.

"Will and consciousness are our VORTEX" --
surely here we encounter a new element. What sort
of vortex has the author in his mind? The familiar
cosmological images -- tree, rose, waterspout -- no
longer stand alone. No thing is only its material.
It is also what we understand it to be. When something enters our perception, it "matters" to us.
Instantly, questions of meaning and value arise.

To this point the presiding metaphors have all
been drawn from the natural world; we have sought
the mutual intelligibility -- and as it were permea-
bility -- of language and the articulated patterns
of the living cosmos, one to another. Now we follow
the metamorphosis of these patterns into paradigms
for human conduct. The analysis loses some of its
literary character and takes on a more philosophical
rigor.

The balance discerned in the rhythms and cycles
of the natural world reveals its human dimension:
equity, justice. Precise definition of the word
acquires a personal locus: sincerity. And the
archetypal metaphor of being human is "fleshed out,"
embodied, incarnated: in the ethic of the fu jen,
the great gentleman, whose word and deed coincide.

54

4 <u>Pivot</u>

"He who can totally sweep clean the chalice
of himself can carry the inborn nature of
others to fulfilment.

"Getting thus to the bottom of the natures
of men, one can thence understand the nature
of material things, and this understanding
of the nature of things can aid the transforming and nutritive powers of earth and
heaven (ameliorate the quality of the grain,
for example), and raise man up to be a sort
of third partner with heaven and earth." (1)

<u>Chung Yung</u> (<u>Unwobbling Pivot</u>),
Pound translation

It is in Pound's Chinese studies that we find
the three worlds most explicitly in harmony. Here
the "Great Balance" is maintained. Here the poet
quite graphically "observes a design in the Process"(2), and attunes himself to "the kind of intelligence that enables the grass seed to grow grass
and the cherry-stone to make cherries."

The calm, formal perfection of the Chinese
world as Pound construed it had tremendous aesthetic
repercussions for him and for those around him.(3)
It everywhere penetrates his other concerns.

We may take for example Pound's active interest
in the sculptor Constantin Brancusi(4), whose simple
perfection of organic forms displays a maturity
Gaudier did not live long enough to achieve:

Where Gaudier had developed a sort of
form-fugue or form-sonata by a combination of
forms, Brancusi has set out on the maddeningly
more difficult exploration toward getting all
the forms into one form; this is as long as any
Buddhist's contemplation of the universe or as
any medieval saint's contemplation of the divine
love, as long and even as paradoxical as the
final remarks in the <u>Divina Commedia</u>. It is a
search easily begun, and wholly unending... (5)

55

The "poet as sculptor"(6) and the "sculptor of rhyme" are by now staples of the Pound literature. One might also legitimately invoke Henry Moore, who began his first direct carvings in stone and in wood after reading Pound's Gaudier-Brzeska. In Pound's view, the authentic artisan does not "impose" a form on dumb stone. On the contrary; artist and material co-operate. The god dwells "inside the stone" and is only "released" -- that is to say freed -- by the sculptor's chisel. The mutual "dwelling-within-one-another"(7) of the divinity (here conceived as pure principle) and the world (cosmos, matter, material) has not been sundered; there is yet commerce(8) between dimensions of the real. The artist presides at the threshold of the hidden god's "diaphany." Pound again on Brancusi:

> Above all he is a man in love with perfec-tion. Dante believed in the "melody which most in-centers the soul"; in the preface to my Guido I have tried to express the idea of an absolute rhythm, or at least the possibility of it. Per-haps every artist at one time or another be-lieves in a sort of elixir or philosopher's stone produced by the sheer perfection of his art; by the alchemical sublimation of the me-dium; the elimination of accidentals and imper-fections.(9)

There is much more at stake in Pound's atten-tion to sculpture and the perfection of form than some merely capricious synaesthetic predilection for multi-media effects. Once channels of communication between realms of the real are reopened -- as they were to the Shaman via the cosmic axis of the World Tree, or to the Yogin via the chakras of his spinal cord(10) -- once the conduit is clear, passage be-tween Heaven and Earth becomes not only an abstract possibility, but a fundamental human -- and thereby artistic -- exigency.

We earlier approached this "passage" on another footing; we saw how the eidos, Pound's nonconceptual Image, was in fact logos, i.e. preordinately and preeminently verbal (linguistic and dynamic rather than pictorial and static) in character. Just as this Image turned out to be neither the one picture (faces) nor the other (petals), so too this logos Pound attempts to articulate is not one "word" or another, as might be pinpointed in a dictionary, but

56

a verbal passage -- that is, a dialogue, a dia-logos. The world-view embodied in one language or another is also embedded there, and not sufficiently universal. The search for deeper paradigms begins. And one place the search led Ezra Pound, time and again, was to the Chinese classics.

It can be said that the dialogical character of Pound's poetic is nowhere more striking than in his idiosyncratic approach to the ancient Chinese world -- which is not a unilinear, as it were "academic" study of China, its history and customs(11) -- but instead the creative act of placing this world in dialogue with the more familiar(12) worlds of Homer and Dante. What emerges from Pound's intense scrutiny of the secular religiousness of the Confucian tradition is thus not a battery of historical facts arrayed for purposes of logical proof, but certain regenerative and interaccommodative paradigms for civilized human intercourse which may claim a catholicity far beyond the range of mere historicism.

When we look to his Chinese translations -- "appropriations" might be the better term(13) -- we approach the heart of Pound's ethical vision. It is worth noting that Pound's work as a whole is really the only proper context for evaluating his Chinese translations. Sinologists who continue clucking over his "magnificent misreadings" have themselves misread Pound somewhat less than magnificently. T.S. Eliot, recall, dubbed Pound "Inventor of China" for the 20th century, a turn of phrase which gives Pound's achievement due credit without neglecting the liabilities of such an "original" approach to Chinese scholarship.

Whatever its other merits or demerits, the value of Pound's "invention" of key Chinese texts for his own ongoing project is patent. Pound's persistent faith in the balance -- human, cosmic and divine -- espoused and exemplified by the sages of the Four Books (14) underpins everything he wrote after World War I, including (sadly) the often severely unbalanced political tracts of the late thirties and early forties. On the latter, it may be enough to note that when Pound translated from his captivity at Pisa the Confucian maxim "Attacking false systems only harms you", he spoke from painful experience. As to the politics of the matter, I daresay they are by and large irrelevant -- at least in the long-run. Who today, asked point blank, would be

57

quite certain whether Dante was a Guelph or a Ghibel-
line? It is in the face of the brutal blindness
that conceives the world only in terms of such 180-
degree oppositions and irreconcilable conflicts --
between us and them, right and left, black and
white, etc. -- that poets will ever seek (and sometimes even find) the greater balance:

> Happiness, rage, grief, delight -- to be
> unmoved by these emotions is to stand in the
> axis, in the center; being moved by these pas-
> sions each in due degree constitutes being in
> harmony.

By his own admission, Pound's utterance was not
always so balanced. In his later years he would go
out of his way to repudiate a well-deserved reputa-
tion for ire: "Violent language is ALWAYS a mistake." Just so much more remarkable, then, is his
unbroken faith in the ultimate coherence and eu-
rhythmia of the entire reality. The passage cited
above continues:

> That axis in the center is the great
> root of the universe; that harmony
> is the universe's outspread process [Tao]
> (of existence).

> From this root and in this harmony Heaven
> and Earth are established in their precise
> modalities, and the multitudes of all
> creatures persist, nourished on their
> meridians. (15)

"Nourished on their meridians" -- doubtless some
sinologists would quibble over the choice (a biolo-
gical inspiration?) of "meridians." But Pound took
such values very seriously, and stands or falls in
his own eyes by the standards he set for himself.
Certainly no trumped-up political indictment (16) of
Pound's contorted ranting and raving over Rome radio
during World War II could be so harsh as the "sentence" he subsequently imposed on himself: silence.
For the man, merely a blank epitaph. But for the
poet, a living death...

To summarize, then, by putting mid-20th century
politics to one side (or the other, as you like), in
his Confucian translations Pound allows us access to
certain structures of value he considers normative
and binding on himself, as well as on human affairs

in general. Thus in addition to the cosmological interpatternings we have discussed, it is necessary now to try to gather the sense of this ethical, and hence anthropological paradigm. We shall in short order repair to the texts of some of Pound's Chinese translations. We shall interrogate them mainly for what they have to say to us, and examine how it is they go about being coherent. We shall also have to provide some context, since the tradition itself requires fidelity less to the letter of the text than to the truth of what is being translated. There seems a scarcity of critical tools in the arsenal of western scholarship to deal with this sort of "translation from within," though the pheno-menon(17) is common enough in the history of the great religious literatures.(18) But if the trans-lator is not in some measure actually converted to the truth of what he or she is translating, not only would the translation ring hollow, but there would in all likelihood be no translation at all. Why would one bother?

In Pound's case, moreover, circumstances com-pound the difficulty. He undertook to retranslate some of the texts we shall be considering (e.g., the Chung Yung) during the period of his incarceration -- under indictment for treason in time of war -- in a cage made of airplane scrap, exposed to the ele-ments, at the Military Detention Training Center near Pisa in late 1945. He half-expected to be hung.(19) Pound did have a pocket dictionary with him at Pisa, but none while translating the Ta Hsio eight years prior, as Kenner relates:

...on a six-week retreat in the late sum-mer of 1937 he had no dictionary small enough to pack, and simply stared at the ideograms and the crib. "When I disagreed with the crib or was puzzled by it I had only the look of the characters and the radicals to go from." He went "three times through the whole text," and rose from it "with a better idea of the whole and the unity of the doctrine... the constants have been impressed on my eye." (20)

The "poet as sculptor," the perceiver of form, pat-tern and proportion, had always had other resources. More than 30 years earlier he had seen in the ideo-gram for the "dawn" (albeit with Fenollosa's eyes) the sun tangled in the branches of a tree, and the tone of his translations differs from that of a Legge or a Pauthier accordingly.

In the texts reworked at Pisa, then, instead of literal "correctness" we confront sheer artistry in the face of the artist's imminent demise. These translations from the Stone Books, together with the Pisan Cantos inscribed on facing pages of the same notebook, amount to nothing less than Pound's Testament.(21) Let us not mistake them for something else. Let us attend instead to the "sculptor" in Pound, ever sensitive to metaphorical relativities, who divines the spirit captive in the stone -- and sets it free.

CONFUCIUS' TEXT

1.
        The great learning
(adult study, grinding the corn in
the head's mortar to fit it for use)
takes root in clarifying the way
wherein the intelligence increases
through the process of looking
straight into one's own heart
and acting on the results; it is
rooted in watching with affection
the way people grow; it is rooted
in coming to rest, being at ease
in perfect equity. (22)

In the chapter 'Human Community As Holy Rite' of his Confucius -- The Secular As Sacred, Professor Herbert Fingarette writes:

> The ceremonial act is the primary, irreducible event.

and goes on to point out that we in the West have not yet really understood Confucius' vision of li (usually rendered holy rite, or rites, ritual, sacred ceremony).(1) For Fingarette, and I would suggest for the Confucian translator Ezra Pound, this peculiar blindness on the part of many western sinologists(2) is what has kept us from seeing Confucius as a radical innovator whose insight speaks directly to our day, and instead leads us to caricature the sage as a pompous and platitudinous pedant with puffed-up manners.(3) He thus too easily becomes the butt of ridicule. By contrast, here is Fingarette on li:

> In the well-learned ceremony, each person does what he is supposed to do according to a pattern (li). My gestures are coordinated harmoniously with yours -- though neither of us has to force, push, demand, compel or otherwise "make" this happen. Our gestures are in turn smoothly followed by those of the other participants, all effortlessly. If all are "self-disciplined, ever turning toward li," then all that is needed -- quite literally -- is an initial ritual gesture in the proper ceremonial context; from there onward, everything "happens."

> Confucius characteristically and sharply contrasts the ruler who uses li with the ruler who seeks to attain his ends by means of commands, threats, regulations, punishments and force. (Analects 2:3) The force of coercion is manifest and tangible, whereas the vast (and sacred) forces at work in li are invisible and intangible. Li works through spontaneous coordination rooted in reverent dignity. (4)

This li, then, is no mere law or legalism, not an order imposed; nor is it the mere indifference of anarchic relativism. It is a pattern of coordinated human intercourse which accommodates, and thus persists through, changing circumstances; once again, a fluxus quo, but now with human and ethical repercussions. Underneath Pound's loud political pronouncements one discovers a gentler order of things. It is almost as if some of his better known prejudices were constructed, perhaps quite unconsciously, to protect the more graceful, more balanced Confucian heart of his life-long attention to government and governments.

Certainly Fingarette's clarifications help make more accessible Pound's translation of a crucial Analects passage meant to describe the "gentilesse" in the ways and means of the sage ruler: "The wind blows, the grass bends." What could be more simple? It can be said that human community consists of its "care-structure," in the delicate fabric of day-to-day relations between people, in all that "goes without saying," in the unspoken accord underlying even the homeliest of social exchanges. It is all li:

> Explicitly, Holy Rite is thus a luminous point of concentration in the greater and ideally all-inclusive ceremonial harmony of the perfectly humane civilization of the Tao, or ideal Way. Human life in its entirety finally appears as one vast, spontaneous and holy Rite: the community of man. (5)

The etymology of this most intriguing word li indicates that it first meant simply pattern -- as the grain in the wood, or the markings in jade -- and only eventually came to mean the "pattern of patterns" we find in the Confucian texts. Professor Needham translates it "principle of organization" and comments in his Science and Civilization in China:

> In its most ancient meaning, it [li] signified the pattern in things, the markings of jade or fibers in muscle. ... It acquired the common dictionary meaning "principle," but always conserved the undertone of "pattern." There is "law" implicit in it, but this law is the law to which parts of wholes have to conform by virtue of their very existence as parts of wholes. (6)

It is Fingarette who best explicates the perception that this most <u>universal</u> of patterns (<u>li</u>) is always and only <u>concrete</u>:

I see you on the street; I smile, walk toward you, put out my hand to shake yours. And behold -- without any command, stratagem, special tricks or tools, without any effort on my part to make you do so, you spontaneously turn toward me, return my smile, raise your hand toward mine. We shake hands -- not by my pulling your hand up and down or your pulling mine but by spontaneous and perfect cooperative action. Normally we do not notice the subtlety and amazing complexity of this coordinated "ritual" act. This subtlety and complexity become very evident, however, if one has had to learn the ceremony from a book of instructions, or if one is a foreigner from a nonhandshaking culture. (7)

In Pound's digest: "Aim of law is to prevent coercion." Deference, not dominance, establishes and maintains human(e) community. When the ceremony is performed in perfect spontaneity rooted in reverent dignity, "It just happens." It is the opposite of the mechanical or perfunctory ritualism for which it has carelessly been mistaken. This in mind, note how Pound renders the culminating verse of Tsze Tsze's Second Thesis: "He who understands the meaning and the justice of the rites to Earth and Heaven will govern a kingdom as if he held it lit up in the palm of his hand."(8) Just so, Fingarette cites a famous instance from the <u>Analects</u>, 15:4: "The Emperor sat facing south [as was ritually proper] and everything [duly] took place." (9) And from Pound's Canto 99 (p. 698), even more fluidly:

The sages of Han had a saying:
Manners are from earth and from water
They arise out of hills and streams
The spirit of air is of the country
        Men's manners can not be one
              (same, identical)
Kung said: are classic of heaven,
They bind thru the earth
                    and flow
With recurrence...

*   *   *

All the preceding should serve to define the ceremonial act, li, the sacrament of human community itself. Now we shall turn our attention to the actor, the fu jen, the great gentleman, and attempt to understand his role in this sacred drama. (10)

*　　　*　　　*

The striking novelty of the Confucian intuition is that it nips in the bud the dichotomy between human subject and objective world so deeply entrenched in western thought. That we do not but vaguely perceive this radical vision through the veil of our own cultural schizophrenia is another matter. We have learned that the mandate of the "primary, irreducible" ceremonial act is pure spontaneity, a process known by and large in the classics as The Great Learning (Ta Hsio). It is most directly articulated in the book that bears its name as:

> Looking straight into one's own heart
> and acting on the results. (11)

The text further states:

> These two activities constitute the
> process [Tao] which unites outer and inner,
> object and subject, and thence constitutes a
> harmony with the seasons of earth and heaven.
> (12)

In the initial section of the Ta Hsio, traditionally considered the only part of the text actually from the hand of Master Kung, we are given a step-by-step phenomenology of how this spontaneity comes to harmonize outer and inner, object and subject. This is the core of it. In so many words, this is the Great Learning. First the thrust inward, through to the very center:

> (1:4) The men of old wanting to clarify and
> diffuse throughout the empire that light which
> comes from looking straight into the heart and
> then acting, first set up good government in
> their own states; wanting good government in
> their own states, they first established order
> in their own families; wanting order in the
> home, they first disciplined themselves; desiring self-discipline, they rectified their
> own hearts; and wanting to rectify their
> hearts, they sought precise verbal definitions

66

of their inarticulate thoughts (the tones given
off by the heart); wishing to attain precise
verbal definitions, they set to extend their
knowledge to the utmost. This completion of
knowledge is rooted in sorting things into
organic categories.

Then, the return:

(1:5) When things had been classified in organic categories, knowledge moved toward fulfillment; given the extreme knowable points,
the inarticulate thoughts were defined with
precision (the sun's lance coming to rest on
the precise spot verbally). Having attained
this precise verbal definition [aliter, this
sincerity], they then stabilized their hearts,
they disciplined themselves; having attained
self-discipline, they set their own houses in
order; having order in their own homes, they
brought good government to their own states;
and when their states were well government, the
empire was brought into equilibrium.

(1:6) From the Emperor, Son of Heaven, down to
the common man, singly and all together, this
self-discipline is the root.

(1:7) If the root be in confusion,
nothing will be well governed. (13)

Such a text, quite obviously, speaks for itself. It should be noted that one is not convinced
one really understands it unless one has been able
to put the whole of it into practice. (For purposes
of this study, perhaps an ardent attempt at precise
verbal definitions will suffice.) It may be enough
then simply to say that in such a vision, the person
is not segregated from the entire reality (not indi-
vidualized, atomized, alienated). The person is
only the nexus, the knot in the net of relationships
which at once constitutes and sanctifies human community.

The word used in the tradition to characterize
this fullness of the person is jen. The ideogram is
written thus: 仁 , and Pound has glossed it: "Huma-
nitas, humanity, in the full sense of the word..."(14)
Here the person is seen over against the backdrop of
li, the fabric of human reciprocity. "I am myself

67

and my circumstance," as José Ortega y Gasset would have understood the situation.(15)

But Master Kung rarely speaks of jen. He does not see much of it about, and mainly points out what it is not. It is for example not yu, not "troubled." After warning us of the danger of "psychologizing" Kung's notion of jen -- which would only disrupt the balance between the subjective and the objective that IS the Great Learning -- Professor Fingarette has this to say about yu and jen:

> ...the characteristic of being yu, whose absence is critically characteristic of the jen man, is the condition of a person involved in and responding to an objectively unsettled, troubled situation where a bad outcome is a distinct and evident possibility.

> It follows that the absence of yu is the condition of a man who is responding in a way that is well integrated into an objectively settled and organized situation.

> Since li is that structure of human conduct that harmonizes the doings of all men and establishes their well-being as men, it is clear that he who is fully established in li is living a life that is perfectly organized and is entirely conducive to the flowering of human existence.(16)

And elsewhere, as if by definition:

> He who can submit himself to li is jen. (17)

So, in brief: The action, the ceremony, the "primary, irreducible event" is li. The actor, the person, the man and his full content of humanity, is jen. Jen is by no means a psychological state; it is "the shaping of oneself in li." The two constitute a unity, an integral process, a dynamic balance which Fingarette characterizes as a sort of "vector equilibrium":

> Jen is the complete and concentrated power of the separate vectors -- perfect loyalty, good faith, complete respect for human dignity, and so on. Each of these, in turn, is not an inner state (as the western mentalist bias tends to portray it) but a virtue [te] in the original

sense -- a power emanating from the person, a vector of human power. (18)

Pound often stressed this sense of la virtú; for him it can best be described as:

> ...the potency, the efficient property of a substance or person. Thus modern science shows us radium with a noble virtú of energy.(19)

It is enough for us now to note the extent to which Pound has incorporated the Confucian ethos into his translation; the Confucian paradigms in fact transform him, and his words register the depth and authenticity of that conversion.(20) It is precisely because he refuses to remain a detached spectator that Pound's "non-literal" translation of Confucius (with facing-page Chinese) has been assessed, by Achilles Fang and others, as the one most faithful to the tradition.

> Kung said: Hui's mode of action was to seize the unwavering axis, coming to an exact equity; he gripped it in his fist, and at once started using it, careful as if he were watching his chicken coup, and he never let go or lost sight of it. (21)

Perhaps here a short selection from the 'Temple Odes of Chou' (translated in Pound's Confucian Odes) might shed more light than any protracted analysis abstracted from it.

The Temple Odes of Chou*

I

Wholesome and clean the temple space
with health and clarity of the grain;
ordered the harmony and pace
that gentlemen sustain assembled,
gathering what King Wen's virtue sowed,
that is frankness of heart,
straight act that needs no goad.

He who is gone beyond is now the norm in sky,
the map and movement whereto these conform;
as is above, below,
not manifest, incarnate from our sires in span;
needs not dart forth, but is here present in man.

II

Tensile is heaven's decree
in light and grain without end.
As the pure silk (that tears not)
was the insight of Wen,
and he acted upon it.
In its beauty are we made clear,
its beauty is our purification
                as we bow at the altar.
Be strong his line to the fourth generation
may his great-grandsons be strong.

III

Clear, coherent and splendid,
King Wen's dissociations,
continuing use hath perfected,
they are bound in the felicitous program of Chou.

ALITER

Fluid in clarity,
from mouth to ear binding, scintillant;
scrupulous, enkindling,
King Wen's classifications initially
tracing the lines of our worship,
the spirit moves in their use;
hath brought them to focus.
Chou maintained their enlightenment.

71

[IV ...]

Most manifest the insight that goes into action
in forming the whole state service,
thus the kings of old pass not into oblivion.

ALITER

The unviolent (or unwrangling) man
shall the four coigns obey,
whose lucid thought is in act, not in display.
on his instructions many princes form,
nor shall oblivion wreck this norm.

"Kung said: There is an analogy
between the man of breed and
The archer.

"The archer who misses the bull's-
eye turns and seeks the cause of
his failure in himself." (1)

In his scrupulous attention to the "shape" of
Chinese ideograms, Pound claimed he could discern "a
man's character in every brushstroke."(2)   "I believe in technique as the test of a man's sincerity," he wrote in his 'Credo.'(3)   These criteria
lead him to a unique translation of the ideogram
誠 (cheng), generally rendered sincerity, or puri-
ty of heart, or right intent.   For Pound, good
intentions are not enough.   They must be carried
into action.   Thus he defines the Confucian sincerity as precise verbal definitions, and his authority
as a translator from the Chinese has been challenged
on just this point.   This is going too far, critics
complain.   It is not only tautological to define
sincerity as precise definitions, it is not even
precise.   The right-hand element of this ideogrammatic compound is there exclusively for its sound
value;   only a rank amateur or a poet would try to
squeeze meaning out of it... Or so the argument
goes.

Readers more favorable to Pound have pointed
out that there are at least a score of characters in
Chinese which, if affixed to the radical 言 --
meaning "word" when it stands alone -- would produce
the same sound when pronounced.   Why should this
particular one -- meaning "to perfect" or, in
Pound's surmise: "bring to focus" -- be affixed and
not some other?   Since the Genius of the Language
cannot be brought forward to testify, the pedestrian
reader of Pound, unversed in subtleties of the Chinese language, is left to fend for himself as to
what it all means.   On the second part of Pound's
idiosyncratic definition -- "the sun's lance coming
to rest on the precise spot verbally" -- Kenner is
immensely helpful.(4)

But for the main point -- sincerity: precise
verbal definitions -- I would submit that what might
well prove a stumbling-block for a student of an-

cient Chinese lexicography is really a secondary
issue for a reader of Pound. In the context of
Pound's work, the translation is perfectly intelligible and consistent.

Taking his lead from pictorial elements in the
character, Pound offers us not empty syllogistic
tautology but manifest verbal integrity. There is
no sleight-of-hand. Pound is simply doing what he
is talking about at the same time and in the same
words as he is talking about it. It is a sincere
definition of sincerity; a qualified tautology.
There is no remove. There is no subject standing
over against the object of his study. Here, instead, a man's word and his deed coincide. And with
this pivotal definition, the cheng ming, the "rectification of terminology" is suddenly no longer the
sort of dead-letter pedantry one might have supposed
it to be, but is reanimated as the lynchpin of the
entire Confucian ethical system:

Sincerity, this precision of terms
is heaven's process.

What comes from the process
is human ethics. (5)

Certain passages long opaque to westerners are
now shot through with abundant lucidity. In Tsze
Tsze's Third Thesis (of the Chung Yung), for example, we find the following thunderbolt:

Only the most absolute sincerity
under heaven can effect any change
(in things, in conditions). (6)

Any change? Without Pound's translation of
sincerity, I should say that such a statement would
remain vacuous, if not utterly incomprehensible.
The entire text of the Third Thesis is rendered
luminous in such a powerful way that I feel compelled to exhibit the crucial parts of it. (Exhibit
follows this chapter.) Meantime, we should note how
Professor Fingarette addresses this issue of language:

From this standpoint, it is easy to see
that not only motor skills must be learned but
also correct use of language. For correct use
of language is constitutive of effective action... Correct language is not merely a useful

adjunct; it is of the essence of executing the ceremony.

...From this perspective we see that the famous Confucian doctrine of cheng ming, the "rectification of terms" or "correct use of terminology," is not merely an erroneous belief in word-magic or a pedantic elaboration of Confucius' own concern with teaching tradition. (7)

Fingarette parallels to the cheng ming of Master Kung Professor J. L. Austin's notion of performative utterance. (8) When you say "I do" at your marriage ceremony, you really do. This act of giving your word is itself performative: your word is your deed. You are thus an honest man, a fu jen, a gentleman, a man of your word. Given such an intuition, it is perhaps not difficult to understand why Professor Austin eventually came to believe that all utterance was originally performative. And Pound? Speaking now from a madhouse in Virginia:

What Confucius has to say about style is contained in two characters. The first says "Get the meaning across," and the second says "Stop." (9)

Hugh Kenner, who reports the incident, follows up:

And on being asked what was in the character "Get the meaning across," [Pound replied] "Well, some people say I see too much in these characters"-- here a goodnatured glance at ambient lunatics -- "but I think it means" -- the Jamesian pause -- "'Lead the sheep out to pasture'." (10)

Here we may be glimpsing the way such an intuition is to be carried into practice. How is this verbal ethic to be rooted so that it is not merely a matter of individualistic whim or caprice on the one hand, or merely an order imposed, a new law or ideology on the other?

"Lead the sheep out to pasture..." As Fingarette points out, Confucius himself leapt vertically over such nominalist pitfalls in his use of the mythic narrative.(11) Recall, as Pound constantly does, that Confucius was the first editor of the

75

Odes, a distillation of songs sung of, by, and in honor of, the ancestors; and he set them to music as well, though none of his scores have come down to us. In these poems, the "sage kings of antiquity" and the commoners alike present themselves as, so to speak, a parallel world (if we understand that parallels eventually converge), much as Pound in his turn attempted to present Kung's world parallel to our own. It is the mythic dimension of such an intuition which brings it home in a way no intellectual elucubration ever could. Pound knew this all too well: "An appeal to reason is about a 13% appeal to reality."(12)

The myth itself, strictly speaking, is what is not said in the words of such a narrative; it is the mute(13) dimension of human community, the horizon of tacit accord over against which anything and everything makes whatever sense it makes to us. In the Confucian world, the mythic narrative has to be seen as if transcribed on the background matrix of li. Without this "pattern of patterns," The Odes may be interesting for their little stories, or as a compendium of folklore, but they are hardly intelligible to us as the backbone of a new and total social ethos. Fingarette remarks the notable point that for us today, "What we call history is, so to speak, our myth."(14) History is our touchstone of truth, the reference grid to which we refer facts in order that they become meaningful to us -- and so, as is the way with living myths, we take our myth of history utterly for granted and criticize the "primitive myths" of others by appealing to history...

The mythic narrative succeeds in unifying divergent philosophical opinions because it is constitutively susceptible to a plurality of interpretations. Not so with concepts. My concept is my conception, i.e., mine and not yours. We might argue the point... My myth I do not even notice until my neighbor takes the trouble to point up something I am taking for granted. The myth is the context for any text; it is the cultural horizon provided me by my expectations (future) and my contemporaries (present), but above all by my tradition (past). Thus we begin to understand how it is that Confucius' attention to tradition comes as a radical innovation, rather than as some sort of polemical nostalgia. The Warring States period in which he lived was a troubled time. The Legalists were burning books to enforce their break with the past... (15)

But Confucius chose instead to root his new approach
to humane civilization in a painstaking reinterpreta-
tion of the "ancestors" and the "parallel" Chou
world. He "made it new," and thus from its incep-
tion the Confucian is a tradition of renewal. In
this sense, Pound's work 25 centuries later can be
located smack in the center of that tradition.(16)
Even so, it was perhaps premature:

> The great balance is not made in a day,
> nor for one holiday only. (17)

The fact is that even today it is difficult for
us to assess Confucius -- he goes farther than we are
prepared to go. In his sacralization of the secular, of the fabric of common custom that really
constitutes humane community, Confucius so thoroughly
refuses to either objectivize or subjectivize the
real that the wholistic character of his vision can
only be obscured if we insist on approaching it, in
customary scholarly fashion, from either of these
partial perspectives.

We tend nowadays to be more receptive to explicit critiques than implicit ones, but the upshot of
the Great Learning is simply that subject and object, the jen man and the ceremonial act, inner and
outer, the "psychological" and the "sociological,"
are in fact one process.

The balance between Man and Cosmos is for Kung
the mandate of Heaven itself: destiny. That the
subjective and the objective are two poles of the
real, or "shores" washed by the same river, if you
like, indeed; but they do not exhaust that reality.
There is always more to it... There is always also
the exquisite relativity of Man and World, the way
they are "fitting" together -- which is not some
"other thing," but rather their poise, their constant and delicate balancing and interaccommodation.
This is the Great Learning: "Looking straight into
one's own heart" (the thrust into subjectivity,
idealization), and "acting on the results" (the
thrust into objectivity, realization). It is just
this dynamic balance, this "vector equilibrium,"
this tensional integrity which we have come to recognize as the Tao of Master Kung. The most worthy
translation may indeed be Pound's process, which
sacrifices neither the flux nor the "shape" it
takes.

It is notable that by the time of Chu Hsi and the Neo-Confucians (12th century CE), not only had a full-scale metaphysic evolved out of the "sincerity" of the Chung Yung(18), but also that, considered in the light of what was to come of it, Master Kung is even more apophatic about the divine than the Buddha about nirvāna.(19) There is no question: "Heaven is Heaven."(20) Pound liked to cite what is reputedly the entire text of a lecture once delivered by a Confucian scholar to a western congress of philosophy:

> Gentlemen from the West:
> Heaven's process is quite coherent,
> And its main points perfectly clear. (21)

Nor is there in the primordial texts any elaboration of this Tao of Heaven per se. Its integrity is everywhere manifest. What we may glean from this is that the coherence of the entire reality is not something "else" added to the sheer relativity of Man and Cosmos; it is only, so to speak, their belonging together... not as antagonists, surely, nor in some contrived master/slave relation, nor yet in some bland and homogenized uniformity; but rather by virtue of their very being, Man and the Earth are already "bespoken" one to the other as partners in the audacious creative freedom Kung calls the mandate of Heaven.

When this center no longer holds, when the old Gods are eclipsed and the new as yet unborn, when things fall asunder and every value is turned on its head, then -- and perhaps only then -- the healing vision of the whole surfaces again spontaneously, almost effortlessly, with all the gentle persistence of destiny.

In Pound's words from Pisa:

> What you depart from
> is not the way... (22)

TSZE SZE'S THIRD THESIS*

XXI

Intelligence that comes from sincerity is called
nature or inborn talent; sincerity produced by reason is called education, but sincerity [this activity which defines words with precision] will create
intelligence as if carved with a knife-blade, and
the light of reason will produce sincerity as if
cut clean with a scalpel.

XXII

Only the most absolute sincerity under heaven
can bring the inborn talent to the full and empty
the chalice of the nature.

He who can totally sweep clean the chalice of
himself can carry the inborn nature of others to its
fulfillment; getting to the bottom of the natures of
men, one can thence understand the nature of material
things, and this understanding of the nature of
things can aid the transforming and nutritive powers
of earth and heaven [ameliorate the quality of the
grain, for example] and raise man up to be a sort of
third partner with heaven and earth.

XXIII

He who does not attain to this can at least cul-
tivate the good shoots within him, and in cultivating
them arrive at precision in his own terminology,
that is, at sincerity, at clear definitions. The
sincerity will begin to take form; being formed it
will manifest; manifest, it will start to illumi-
nate, illuminating to function, functioning to effect changes.

Only the most absolute sincerity under heaven
can effect any change [in things, in conditions].

XXIV

In the process of this absolute sincerity one can
arrive at a knowledge of what will occur. Kingdoms
and families that are about to rise will give,
perforce, happy indications; kingdoms and families
about to decay will give forth signs of ill augury.
You look at the divining grass and at the turtle's
shell; but look at the four limbs.

79

If ill fortune or good be on the way, one or the
other, the good will be recognizable before hand,
the ill will be evident before hand, and in this
sense absolute sincerity has the power of a spiritual being, it is like a numen.

XXV

1.

He who defines his words with precision will
perfect himself and the process of this perfecting
is in the process [that is, in the process [Tao] par
excellence defined in the first chapter, the total
process of nature].

2.

Sincerity is the goal of things and their origin, without this sincerity nothing is.
On this meridian the man of breed respects, desires sincerity, holds it in honor and defines his
terminology.

3.

He who possesses this sincerity does not lull
himself to somnolence perfecting himself with ego-
centric aim, but he has a further efficiency in
perfecting something outside himself.
The inborn nature begets this activity naturally, this looking straight into oneself and thence
acting. These two activities constitute the process
which unites outer and inner, object and subject,
and thence constitutes a harmony with the seasons of
earth and heaven.

XXVI

1.

Hence the highest grade of this clarifying activity has no limit, it neither stops nor stays.

2.

Not coming to a stop, it endures; continuing
durable, it arrives at the minima [the seeds whence
movement springs].

3.

From these hidden seeds it moves forth slowly
but goes far and with slow but continuing motion it
penetrates the solid, penetrating the solid it comes
to shine forth on high.

4.

   With this penetration of the solid it has effects upon things, with this shining from on high,
that is with its clarity of comprehension, now here,
now yonder, it stands in the emptiness above with
the sun, seeing and judging, interminable in space
and in time, searching, enduring, and therewith it
perfects even external things.

5.

   In penetrating the solid it is companion to the
brotherly earth [offers the cup of mature wine to
the earth], standing on high with the light of the
intellect it is companion of heaven persisting in
the vast, and in the vast of time, without limit
set to it.

6.

   Being thus in its nature; unseen it causes harmony; unmoving it transforms; unmoved it perfects.

7.

   The celestial and earthly process can be defined
in a single phrase; its actions and its creations
have no duality. [The arrow has not two points.]
   There is no measuring its model for the creation
of things.

<u>tse pu ts'e</u>

8.

   The celestial and earthly process pervades and
is substantial; it is on high and gives light, it
comprehends the light and is lucent, it extends
without bound, and endures.

man standing by his word

81

C/ Theological Transparencies;

Ezra Pound's Paradiso

We have come some distance toward a fuller
understanding. We have made at least one fundamental discovery: The theological dimension is not
something "else" added on to the constitutive relativity of Man and Cosmos.

Similarly, it is clear that Ezra Pound's "Paradiso" is not some "other thing" added on to the
dimensions of his poetic we have so far examined.
The paradise might better be understood as the depth
dimension pertaining and perduring between all the
cosmological and anthropological relativities we
have already encountered; the common integrity of
all those Betweens. One might indeed go so far as
to declare that this depth dimension permeates the
whole of Pound's work to such an extent that no
single passage or "block" of Cantos exhausts the
sheer luminosity Pound associates with Heaven.

The idea did however enter Pound's mind (in
Pisa first, naturally, then at St. Elizabeth's) that
he was winding up his life's poem, that he had
passed thematically from the Inferno of the first
thirty Cantos, through the Purgatorio of the Chinese
and American Cantos, and now (especially after crossing "over Lethe" at Pisa) would continue the journey, as Dante had before him, through the luminous
spheres of his own Paradiso. He does in fact break
into what Hugh Kenner has called a "syncretic exaltation"* from time to time, but the long-awaited
culmination, crescendo or whatever failed him, or he
fell short of it. "I botched it," he would say in
the late sixties, and many who had never really
understood his project in the first place leapt on
the opportunity to pronounce his work a failure.
Nonetheless, the attempt is notable. The task of a
Paradiso may well be implausible or impossible in
our time, as many have suggested, but we shall
examine in Chapter 7 the extent to which such a
quest resonates with the perennial vocation of the
poet.

Insofar as "Heaven is Heaven," then, it is to
be found in Pound's work as a whole. Insofar as
Pound was (somewhat selfconsciously) "writing a
Paradiso" in his later years**, however -- for which
presumption he apologizes in Canto CXX -- there are

certain structural tangencies with Dante's _Paradiso_
and the Neo-Platonic metaphysic of light.   In Chapter 8, the question of structure and coherence will
be taken up into an exposition of some of the principles underlying Pound's sense of order.   The tangencies with the "celestial hierarchies" of Dante
and St. Denys will be charted in Chapter 9.

7 The Poetic Vocation

> "By the ten mouths
> of the tradition:
> Have peace." (1)

a/ The Poet's Calling

Perennially the "calling" of poet is a mystery,
certainly no less so in the bustle of modernity than
it has been down the ages. Poetry seems an "uncal-
led for" and unprofitable avocation (unless one
writes "hits" for the "recording industry"), and the
poet a useless superfluity. In an aggressively
anti-literate era like our own age of television
uniquack, it is barely a tolerable eccentricity to
bother reading poems, let alone writing them. To
the popular mind, the whole business smacks of ob-
noxious elitism. There is much that has been forgotten, or misunderstood, about the poet's calling.
Advertising limericks and computer "prophecies"
monopolize the public eye and ear. We feel bereft
of criteria; what is the genuine article? Perhaps
we should pause to take our bearings.

First of all, there is much about the vocation
of poet that must by rights remain mysterious. There
is an initiation to be gone through, a "terrible
trial" -- personal, social, spiritual -- that is as
Upward's afflicted Genius reminded Pound(2), more
than reminiscent of the awakening of the shaman to
his sacred calling in primordial religious traditions. It is, undeniably, an experience of death,
dismemberment, dissolution... and then, miraculous-
ly, of rebirth, resurrection, reintegration. This
journey to the wellsprings of life, and back again,
may be nothing less than the archetypal religious
experience of humankind: the same motif appears in a
thousand different climes, cultures and costumes;
its antiquity is evidenced by the shaman in trance
depicted on the Lascaux cave walls; its contempora-
neity by the Mass celebrated daily in your neigh-
borhood church. In the context of shamanism proper,
however, it is important to bear in mind that most
often both the death and the rebirth actually occur,
as performance, in the mimetic song the shaman/poet
sings before the community. The song is precisely
the medium of shamanic flight -- through the air,
and between the generations. Shamanic song "re-collects" all the elements of the journey, and thus of
the entire reality. In recounting his or her pas-

sage from death to life, the shaman is also putting the world back together again. Only thus is the Great Healing accomplished: personal transformation and world renewal coalesce in the song of the shaman.

Mircea Eliade has amassed a great deal of lore about the process in his classic Shamanism(3), but has not explicitly considered how shamanism might come to light in the contemporary world. Indeed, his technique of pitting the sacred against the profane in a historical dialectic may inhibit him from registering the equally real appearance of the sacred in the midst of the secular.(4) Living shamans have steadily been adding their testimony to the findings of the scholars; the material available ranges from Black Elk's classical account of the visions of a Sioux heyhoka(5) to Carlos Castenada's provocative apprenticeship with a Yaqui sorceror.(6) We may readily disagree as to how much weight to give one sort of report vis-à-vis another, but there is plainly a genuine religious phenomenon here, and one not entirely absent from our pragmatic modern world.

Still, we are ambivalent about this poet/shaman. We no longer take his or her word for granted as "revelation," pure and simple, as our ancestors might have done. But neither can we any longer justify the brusque dismissal of visionary states as psychosocial "aberrations" best treated in mental hospitals like the one where Pound was confined for twelve years. We are beginning murkily to respect the lucidity whence poetic "rapture" issues; we sense some of the contours -- the heights and depths, at least -- of the visionary landscape common to sorcerors, seers, prophets, mystics and poets. And we are learning, if ever so slowly, to discover intelligibility where our "scientific" mentality once conveniently supposed only confusion and ignorance to reign. But the poetic vision still seems somehow removed from our lives, "not of this world," a fantasy from the childhood of Man, a strange land where all who enter do so as strangers. By what compass are we to orient ourselves in this terra incognita?

The tripartite world of the shaman/poet has been much discussed in learned circles during the past two decades.(7) We are quite conversant with the rites of passage, the tree or pillar at the navel of the Earth, and the psychopomp's ascent or

descent by means of this "axis mundi" into the celestial or infernal regions. We have pieced together
much evidence. We know very well that the "heavens"
visited by shamans from the most diverse quarters of
the globe are customarily arranged in a numbered
hierarchy -- nine levels, most often, or seven, or
sometimes ten.(8) But we no longer have any context
for these data. We cannot be sure what it all means.
From the myriad fragments of our archaeological,
historiographic and ethnological evidence, many
scholars in the field are still unable to synthesize
a meaningful ensemble. We are able to say with
authority that the Eskimo world, or the Yakut universe, or a Gothic cathedral, or the Cretan laby-
rinth, was structured in thus and such a way, but we
are somehow still unable to assimilate these ultimate horizons into our own lives and world-views.(9)

     And so we continue to "generate data" about
other cultures, other world-views, and at the same
time to bemoan the loss of meaning and coherent
values in our own. Where is the bridge between "us"
and "them"? What meaning has the "ecstatic" tradition of visionary flight for the flat world of day-
to-day business? How do you get there ("B") from
here ("A")?

     It is for just such a momentous "leap" that the
poet is called, and called forth. It is the person
of the poet that bridges the apory between our
"knowledge" of traditions where we may trace coherent human meaning and value, and the wisdom we so
sorely need to discover that meaning and that value
in the helter-skelter jumble of modernity. Out of
this need, the poet is called forth.(10) Out of
this lack, he or she creates (or rather co-creates)
a thread, a bridge, a path of meaning "wide as a
hair..."(11), on which tightrope we are all challenged to find and keep a precarious balance.

     Let us say then that the poet's calling is a
double one. The human need for meaning and value
calls for a poet, a "maker." And the poet in his or
her turn is called by the tradition of meaning to
which he or she -- and each of us, in dim imcompre-
hension -- is heir. In a certain sense it is thus
the language itself, "the dialect of the tribe,"
that "treasure house" of meaning, the "mother tongue,"
so to speak, that calls the poet to his or her
perennial task.
                  *   *   *

b/ The Poets Who Call

Nor is this all. The "mother tongue"(12) calls to the poet in the voices of those it has called before. The "Genius"(13) of a given language seems often to lie dormant, for centuries sometimes, falling into cliché and redundancy. Then it awakens, often quite suddenly; it flares up, it is manifest. Something happens. A true poet enters, sings his or her song, and the world of meaning and value is transfigured. The "Genius" of the language is so to speak "personified," embodied in the voice of a Homer, a Dante, a Li Po, a Sappho, a Kalidasa or a Chaucer.(14) The "classical" poet is the one who sings with such grace, or freedom, or beauty that the next poet is called -- and thus called forth -- by that voice, stirred from slumber and awakened to new voice, new song, new meaning. As Hölderlin (15) had it:

Much, from the morning onwards,
Since we have been a discourse
          and have heard from one another,
Has humankind learnt; but soon
                    we shall be song. (16)

Very simplistically, this is one way to approach what Ezra Pound understood by "the tradition." He heard as it were voices, voices which stirred him to raise his own, to lift the song into new phrasings, new cadences, new figures of meaning for his own world. This is why translation became for him the paradigmatic poetic.(17) "Blood for the ghosts," as Hugh Kenner noted(18): In the pulsebeat of the living poet dwell the shades of his illustrious ancestors. In Pound's "voice," truly a chorus can be heard, dimly rustling and restless at first, then clamoring to be heard, vying with one another for audience, and finally articulating distinct but not incompatible words.(19)

Here we approach the substance of Canto I, which we left in suspended animation at the end of Part I. The ghosts crowd round Odysseus, each seeking voice again through the power of the blood sacrifice. And, after he has first heard Tiresias -- read Homer, blind seer himself -- Odysseus allows them to speak. Note that in Pound's edited version of Book XI, only Tiresias' voice comes through, and only a snatch of his speech is preserved. The voices of the others -- Anticlea, Iphimedea, Echenous,

Alkinous, Agamemnon, even that of Achilles -- all
seem to have faded away.(20) And what remains of Tiresias' speech is ominous: "Odysseus shalt return
through spiteful Neptune... lose all companions."(21)

Yet in this primordial Underworld scene we may
glimpse something of what a poet is, or discerns
himself to be -- a clear place, a sort of conduit
between dimensions of the real, as it were an "opening"... Into this "hollow tube"(22), the breath of
the tradition pipes a polyphonic symphony.

We read Pound and are at first all too discon-
certed by the many "references" (most of which have
been annotated by diligent scholarship over the past
30 years(23)), but we tend not to notice immediately
that here Homer speaks, and there Dante; here Kung
calls us again to the rites, or Erigena to the light
divine.

Although the "10 voices of the tradition" speak
through Pound's voice, they are distinct from it.
He generally even presents patches of the original
languages. And we know Pound's "yatter" is something else again -- at best the griping, cantankerous
and authoritarian cracker-barrel philosopher; at
worst the angry, vicious Rome radio propagandist
still unforgiven by many who heard him. But the
voices which speak through Pound are altogether
different and more precious. They temper his own
flaws with a grace and subtle beauty quite incompar-
able in 20th century letters.

It is, then, in these congruences with the
living voices of several traditions -- and in the
creative freedom with which he allows them to flower
anew in his work -- that we shall find Ezra Pound's
Paradiso. In a certain sense, only his Inferno was
entirely of his own devising.

*   *   *

c/ The Call

Yet there is still more to reading Pound's later work than hearing in it the voices of his "illustrious ancestors."(24) Behind the "10 voices of the tradition" there is another, deeper and, strangely, silent voice: the calling of what Pound calls "the Beloved," or the "Goddess," "Reina," and so on. All, in short, that a lame reader might be content to describe as Pound's "Muse." However, as Pound himself remarked of the "love songs" of the Provençal troubadors:

> This sort of canzone is a ritual. It must be conceived and approached as ritual. It has its purpose and its effect. These are different from those of simple song. They are perhaps subtler. They make their revelations to those who are already expert.(25)

Unlike Dante's Beatrice, Pound's "Beloved" never speaks. Which is odd. He invokes her often, expresses gratitude, lingers in awe over her eyes, over the mercy that flows from her hands... And yet she never replies in words. Dr. Kenner says that the apparition of the Goddess in the poem always signals "the flux taking form."(26) This probably could not be put more accurately, although some room remains for speculating as to just which form it is that the flux takes...

What Pound calls Beloved is not for him something vague or indifferent; she is at once the personal and the divine dimension of all that Pound reverences. She is the "unknown" beneath every known fact or reference; hers is the "silence" in which the words of his song echo; she is the "space" over against which the pattern is perceived. More than this: If all that is known, shown and spoken in Pound's work could be put in one scale of a balance, she would be the ever mysterious "Other." She is in this sense the necessarily mute dimension to Pound's poetic, the interval, the rhythm structure within which the melody is played, the void over which the drumskin is stretched taut, the terrible abyss at the brink of which the dancers must dance the holy dance. The tradition in all likelihood goes directly back to the Mediterranean matriarchate.(27) Pound knew it through Dante and, behind him, through the Tuscan fideli d'amore(28), and behind them the Provençal troubadors(29), with their

own alchemical admixture of Islamic esoterism(30)
and the chivalric "love code"(31)... The Beloved is
the necessary counterpoint to all that her Lover is;
her grace humbles Pound's occasional lapses into
tastelessness.

In the terms we are suggesting, hers is the
silent call to which Pound's personal calling as
poet responds. By invoking her, he "re-calls" himself. There is ample precedent scattered through
Pound's own critical essays. For example, Pound on
paradise, circa 1912:

> Richard of St. Victor has left us one very
> beautiful passage on the splendors of para-
> dise.(32)

> They are ineffable and innumerable and no man
> having beheld them can fittingly narrate them
> or even remember them exactly. Nevertheless by
> naming over all the most beautiful things we
> know we may draw back on the mind some vestige
> of the heavenly splendor.

> I suggest that the troubador, either more indo-
> lent or more logical, progresses from correlat-
> ing all these details for purpose of compari-
> son, and lumps the matter. The Lady contains
> the catalogue, is more complete. She serves as
> a sort of mantram.(33)

To put a sharp point on it, "She" -- the Beloved,
the Lady, the Goddess, by whatever name -- calls
wordlessly for nothing less than the poet's life.
Through her he is called to the (pro)creative act.
Every genuine creation entails the rite of sacri-
fice(34); but the true sacrifice is to live, not to
die. Thus the poet is called to "give his life" to
her in this way, so that she then may restore the
doomed mortal and, as Leucothea, perhaps, transform
him into a sea-god. Or else, as Artemis, she may
rebuke his importunity by turning her pursuer into a
stag to be devoured by his own hounds. Either way,
the sacrifice must be completed. Her powers should
not be underestimated, nor her stature in Pound's
eyes. In his comments on the Sonnets of Guido
Cavalcanti, Dante's "first friend" and mentor, Pound
writes:

Another line of which Rossetti completely loses
the significance is

"E la beltate per sua Dea la mostra"
(Sonnet VII)

"Beauty displays her for her goddess." That is
to say, as the spirit of God became incarnate
in the Christ, so is the spirit of the eternal
beauty made flesh dwelling amongst us in her.(35)

For Pound she is the most intimate dimension of
mortal life -- she presides over birth, growth and
death. It could only be she who calls for and calls
forth his highest canticle, as Beatrice called Dante
"to write of her what has never been said of any
mortal woman."(36) She is his very predisposition
to the work, the elusive and "inexplicable" state of
mind he so cherishes:

There is, in what I have called the natural course of events, the exalted moment, the
vision unsought, or at least the vision gained
without machination. (37)

And after the event?

nothing matters but the quality
of the affection --
in the end -- and has carved the trace
in the mind (38)

....

Amo ergo sum, and in just that proportion (39)

In short, she IS Pound's poetic vocation. But
perhaps we ought to let him continue speaking for
himself on this point. In the 'Preface' to his
Guido, after defining la virtù as "the potency, the
efficient property of a substance or person," Pound
continues:

The heavens were, according to the Ptolemaic
system, clear concentric spheres with the earth
as their pivot. They moved more swiftly as
they were far removed from it, each one endowed
with its virtue, its property for affecting man
and destiny; in each its star, the sign visible
to the wise and guiding them. A logical astrology, an indication of the position and

movement of that spiritual current. Thus 'her' presence, his Lady's corresponds with the ascendancy of the star of that heaven which corresponds to her particular emanation or potency. Likewise,

"Vedrai la sua virtú nel ciel salita."

thou shalt see the rays of this emanation going up to heaven as a slender pillar of light, or, more strictly in accordance with the stanza preceding, thou shalt see depart from her lips her subtler body, and from that a still subtler form ascends and from that a star, the body of pure flame surrounding the source of the virtú, which will declare its nature.

I would go so far as to say that "Il Paradiso" and the form of "The Commedia" might date from this line. (40)

Nor would it be entirely implausible to suggest that the form of Pound's own attempted "Paradiso" might also trace its lineage from this selfsame presiding intuition. (41)

THE SETTING;

An Interpolation

Excerpt from W.B. Yeats, 'A Packet for Ezra Pound,' in A Vision. After describing the town of Rapallo, Italy, where he visited Pound in 1935:

II

I shall not lack conversation. Ezra Pound, whose art is the opposite of mine, whose criticism commends what I most condemn, a man with whom I should quarrel more than with anyone else if we were not united by affection, has for years lived in rooms opening on to a flat roof by the sea. For the last hour we have sat upon the roof which is also a garden, discussing that immense poem [The Cantos] of which but seven and twenty cantos are already published. I have often found there brightly painted kings, queens, knaves, but have never discovered why all the suits could not be dealt out in some quite different order. Now at last he explains that it will, when the hundredth canto is finished, display a structure like that of a Bach Fugue. There will be no plot, no chronicle of events, no logic of discourse, but two themes, the Descent into Hades from Homer, a Metamorphosis from Ovid, and, mixed with these, medieval or modern historical characters. He has tried to produce that picture Porteous commended to Nicholas Poussin in Le chef d'oeuvre inconnu where everything rounds or thrusts itself without edges, without contours conventions of the intellect -- from a splash of tints and shades; to achieve a work as characteristic of our time as the paintings of Cézanne, avowedly suggested by Porteous, as Ulysses and its dream association of words and images, a poem in which there is nothing that can be taken out and reasoned over, nothing that is not part of the poem itself. He has scribbled on the back of an envelope certain sets of letters that represent emotions or archetypal events -- I cannot find any adequate definition -- A B C D and then J K L M, and then each set of letters repeated, and then A B C D inverted and this repeated, and then a new element X Y Z, then certain letters that never recur, and then all sorts of combinations X Y Z and J K L M and A B C D and D C B A, and all set whirling together. He has shown me upon the wall a photograph of a Cosimo Tura decoration in three compartments, in the upper the Triumph of Love and the Triumph of Chastity, in the middle the Zodiacal signs, and in the lower certain events in Cosimo Tura's day. The Descent and the Metamorphosis -- A B C D and J K L M -- his fixed elements, took the place of the Zodiac, the archetypal persons -- X Y Z -- that of the Triumphs, and certain modern events -- his letters that do not recur -- that of those events in Cosimo Tura's day.

I may, now that I have recovered leisure, find that the mathematical structure, when taken up into imagination, is more than mathematical, that seemingly irrelevant details fit together into a single theme, that here is no botch of tone and colour, all Hodos Chameliontos, except for some odd corner where one discovers beautiful detail like that finely modelled foot in Porteous' disastrous picture.*

"For forty years I have schooled
myself... to write an epic poem
which begins 'In the Dark Forest,'
crosses the Purgatory of human
error, and ends in the light."(1)

a/ Distinctions In Clarity(2)

Pound's poetry does not speak in the way a
philosophical text speaks. Here, as we have just
observed, even the silences are telling. Nor does
Pound's poetry speak in the ways we were, until the
middle of this century, accustomed to hearing poems
speak. Here the rhyme is not a jingle or a swat at
the end of every other line, but rather a consonance
of precise perceptions, as it were a "subject-
rhyme."(3)

There are in Pound's work innumerable references to be deciphered, signs and tags of all sorts
from a dozen languages. But the key to the whole is
not hidden elsewhere; indeed, it is not hidden at
all. Pound once rebuked a would-be extrapolator by
pointing to a Chinese manuscript he had lying about:
"That scroll over there is that scroll over there.
It does not represent something ELSE!"(4) So it is
with The Cantos. The "Beloved," to pick up our
Ariadne's thread, the "Goddess" is not an alias or a
conceit. Nor is she some other person, someone like
Olga Rudge or Marcella Spann whose amorous entangle-
ments with Pound some future biographer might chronicle. Moreover, she is not a "concept," not a
Platonic figure of beauty, for example, abstracted
from this world. Pound himself practically declares
that the Beloved is not to be located elsewhere than
in the poem: "The production IS the Beloved." (5)
Or in Canto 93, where it seems enigmatic: "Beloved,
do not fall apart in my hands."(6) And then a moment later:

You are tender as a marshmallow, my Love.
I cannot use you as a fulcrum.
You have stirred my mind out of dust. (7)

Pound himself was much concerned in his last
years with whether or not his poem "cohered." In
the final Fragments of The Cantos, we find him
lamenting: "M'amour, m'amour, what do I love and

where are you?"(8)   Or: "And I am not a demi-god, I
cannot make it cohere."(9)   Yet on the next page   he
is equally capable of writing: "i.e. it coheres all
right/ even if my notes do not cohere."(10)

Some   have taken snippets like these as   reason
enough to conclude that The Cantos are not in fact a
poem,   but   merely   "notes"   for a   poem.(11)   Noel
Stock(12)   and   others can thus   content   themselves
with accounting Pound's life's work a failure.   But
this is too easy an out.   The poem does make   sense
-- line by line, page by page, image by image.   Hugh
Kenner,   who ought to know,   has testified: "I have
not   found any place where it does not cohere." (13)
But   although   Kenner's   testimony   carries   great
weight,   the   "coherence"   of Pound's "grab-bag"   is
still   hugely problematic for   most   readers.   G.P.
Elliott is perhaps an exaggerated instance:

Do The Cantos have a true structure?   ...a
stable,   rational structure such as the highest
excellence   always   builds and is always   built
upon?   I   think not;   at least I am   not   able
rationally   to   grasp   that order   either   from
studying the poem or any of the exegeses of   it
-- a   disability   I share with all   those   with
whom   I   have discussed the   matter,   including
some whose critical assent only a madman   would
spurn. (14)

Strong   language.   Let us try to untangle some
of these knots.   First of all,   Pound's Cantos   are
songs.   A   song consists precisely of its   "notes."
The structure here is rhythmic, the coherence harmon-
ic.   Certain patterns recur,   certain "images" per-
sist with wave-like regularity.   There is a circular
"pulse-beat" -- Pound spoke of the Great Bass(15) --
governing   the intercourse between dimensions of the
poem. It is not a "solid" structure, not like a wall
of bricks, but then modern physics has discovered no
"solids"   (and for that matter no points,   no lines,
no planes... none,   in short,   of the staples   of
Euclidean geometry) in all universe.   If this were
not the case, if Pound's vision were specialized, or
compartmentalized,   or   its   presentation   strictly
linear,   it   would   be quite impossible   for   us   to
discern   in   the   very presence of the   Goddess   the
common integrity,   and mutual destiny,   of the three
"natures" of the entire reality: cosmic, human and
divine,   keeping to our terminology.(16)

There remains the formidable hemeneutical(17) -- rather than solely exegetical (18) -- task of demonstrating this integrity in a work, namely The Cantos, which measures itself against ultimate criteria different from those to which we are accustomed, in which abide strange deities, elemental creatures and orders of being as it were "alien" to us. Granting that for Pound himself, the Beloved -- her very presence, if we are not mistaken -- seems to indicate the coherence of the whole ("Do not fall apart in my hands"), just where is it that we may find this silent sonority, this mute harmony, these hidden correspondences? How in the Name of Heaven are we to hear the inaudible music of the spheres?

Minimally, it is a question of attunement and alignment with the priorities at issue in the work. Perhaps the dilemma of whether or not Pound's poem makes sense, though eminently soluble, is a somewhat circumscribed way of envisioning the sort of interpretation that is required. The more fundamental question might be whether or not the entire reality coheres as Pound repeatedly attests that it does: "What SPLENDOUR! It all coheres!"(19) Then, next step, we may commence measuring the poem according to its own standards. If we look for systematic philosophy based on an agglomeration of substantives, on nouns only -- as abstract categories, concepts or theses -- Pound's poem would seem to have almost no structural "stability" at all, as Elliott claims. The pyramids were built, we reassure ourselves, by employing what a student of mechanics would term "continuous compression;" blocks piled redundantly on top of other blocks. Pound's poem is certainly not built this way, especially not the latter half of it. It might instead be described as self-suspended structure. Its coherence is tensional rather than compressive, dynamic and verbal rather than agglutinative. In this way the work coheres as one of R. Buckminster Fuller's tensegrity spheres coheres, without any of the compression members ever touching any other. Kenner cites Fuller on this point:

Therefore when nature has very large tasks to do, such as cohering the solar system... she has compression operating in little remotely positioned islands, as high energy concentrations, such as the Earth and other planets, ... while cohering the whole system by continuous tension; compression islands in a nonsimultaneous ocean of tension.(20)

This of course is also Pound's method; nodes of luminous detail in a nonsimultaneous verbal ocean. Kenner adds to Bucky's observation:

> No one can see tension. Newton called one form of it gravity. Another form keeps bicycle wheels from collapsing, and another inhabits the clear spaces on a Japanese scroll.(21)

So it is clear our essay here must not be one of literary criticism alone (as Kenner's is not), nor some sterile exercise in structuralist reductionism. Rather we must effect a genuine fusion of the horizons of meaning offered by these antipodal approaches. There are no short-cuts to an understanding of Pound's work, but some paths are less choked with brambles than others. Hugh Kenner has rightly and for all time legitimized the appeal to Fuller's synergetic geometry in order to clarify how Pound went about making sense.(22) The heuristic models we shall offer in our Illustrations differ somewhat from Kenner's own, but the source is one.(23)

b/ The Celestial Hierarchies

It can be said that Ezra Pound's "Paradiso," customarily understood to comprise the latter half of The Cantos, is difficult for its radical simplicity. As in all Pound's poetry, every word on the page works. There is no "fill," and scant explanation or description of what is going on. The method is one of presentation, not representation. Lightning transitions propel the reader into dense "ideograms" of text, context and texture.(24) Hugh Kenner has called Pound's a "poetic of fact"(25), but since Pound himself demonstrates that poetic facts are interpretive through and through, a case could equally be made that Pound's is a poetic of nuance, undertone and extraordinary subtlety.

The economy of utterance requires a certain sort of reader, one who hears "echoes" in every phrase. When Pound says "Paradiso," for example, he probably has Dante in mind. When he says "Heaven" (T'ien) he follows Kung's lead, he nods in that direction. But he keeps the balance. He knows the differences, as well as the points of possible contact, between the traditions he attempts to fuse. Similarly, the cosmological patterns and anthropological paradigms we have been discussing are aligned and allied with one another throughout Pound's later work. His ethics he derives from watching the plants grow; his metaphysics (often) from the splendor of the sun pouring its tensile radiance into a cloudless heaven. (26) It is above all a poetic of illumination.(27)

And, always, from this delicate balancing act, a new horizon of meaning emerges, a (synergetic) fusion that is more than the sum of its components. The artist in the 20th century employs as it were a broader, or a "deeper" canvas, on which he or she inscribes much more than would be tolerable or even intelligible in a monocultural, or monological, or monochromatic work of art. In Pound's Cantos there are (in planar terms) "levels," or (in a certain theological parlance(28)) "hierarchies," or (in physics, say) "fields" or (quasi-mathematical) "dimensions" which overlap and intertwine and simply cannot be reduced to a single point of view, a single explanation of reality, a single concept, doctrine or ideology. Hence our pluralistic approach. Precisely these diaphanous "cross-over" realities are our concern here; we want to see how the bridges are built.(29)

In R. B. Fuller's terms, which we choose to employ for reasons that should be clarified by the Illustrations, what we are talking about are the frequencies of Pound's "Paradiso."(30) A certain attunement is required to perceive these dimensions in Pound's work. His attention to Dante should for example be documented: Pound first lectured on Dante in 1909(31); thirty years later one would expect him to know this topic very well indeed. Meantime, his most notable public work on Dante was his line-by-line consultation with Laurence Binyon on Binyon's English translation of Il Purgatorio, from which grew the idea proposed in the Letters of a further collaboration on Il Paradiso. (32) The project was abandoned, due to yet another World War, but such background is needed to put the Dantescan emphasis in perspective. Further, one would have to review the way in which Dante derives his own schema of nine heavens and the Empyrean from St. Denys' nine angelic hierarchies(33), and how in turn the Sufi and Shaivite esoteric traditions of Islam had their impact on Dante's world, i.e. how the "angelic hierarchies" came to take up residence in medieval Christendom.(34) Asin Palacios' stubborn claim that Dante's own Paradiso was lifted in toto from Muyaddin Ibn el'Arabi's 'Ascent of Mohammed into Heaven' would have to be evaluated, and presumably laid to rest. But is it not possible that all who journey to these celestial regions, each according to their lights, simply see what is there -- as St. Denys constantly reminds his reader -- "à la mesure de leur forces"(35)?

References abound in the later Cantos to this model of nine heavens, but we need not collate all of them to recognize the pattern. The schema of a hierarchical world of light (be it nine heavens, or seven, or twelve(36)) is a good deal more ancient than human memory, and seems to be as deeply rooted there as the Trinity(37), from which St. Denys explicitly derives his own ninefold vision. St. Denys refers to his angels as the intelligences of their respective spheres, and Pound follows him, taking his cues often from Scotus Erigena(38), the first translator of the Celestial Hierarchies. Fuller would call these governing forms equilibria, per- haps, to emphasize their tensional integrity(39), where Pound would tend to humanize them as "the equities" -- reciprocity, mutuality, deference -- in order to keep the question of justice in focus. But they might both agree that the craft by which one keeps oneself afloat in the flux of this inter-transformative matrix is that of making the proper "distinctions in clarity"(40) at the precise moment and in the proper order. As a poetic method, the process is one of increasing illumination, ephe-meralization(41), spiritualization.

It is not generally assumed that these frequen-cies (or "dimensions," or "hierarchies") are an issue in Pound's own attempt at a Paradiso. Critics often tend to leave the thorny passages as references to some arcane "other world," an ideal realm of some sort(42), or else as indications of some (merely psychological) "state of mind." And there are cer-tainly lines in Pound which do not contradict such conclusions.

It has been our own observation, however, that at the heart of Pound's poetic there is as it were a "clear place," which is to say no "place" at all, but rather an awareness (consciousness is perhaps too selfconscious a word to use here) which is neither wholly Ezra Pound's nor exclusively attribut-able to his many source texts and interlocutors. As Pearlman has noted of The Cantos, "The principle of order at the core of things is an unanalyzable mystery; it is the mystery of the 'dimension of stillness.'"(43)

Given that Pound seeks always the "optimum pre-and con-cision"(44), we must take it as patent that when he says, for example, "Points define a peri-phery"(45), at least two things are happening at once. A periphery is being defined in terms intel-ligible to any Euclidean and, secondly, Pound is making the point that the "main points" in a certain text (in this case The Analects) articulate a far more comprehensive "surround" of meaning.(46) In short, the same set of words conveys a message on more than one level of meaning. It is not polysemy, which would tend toward vapid ambiguity and a con-fusing welter of meanings. Rather, to borrow a term from chemistry, it is the valence of certain quite definite meanings that is at stake in Pound's work, their recombinative power, their ability to adapt intelligibly to new circumstances. Here the words have a certain frequency; they echo, if you will, in the labyrinthine corridors of human and linguistic

memory. To do justice to Pound's poetic, we must
seek out such "nodes" and chart the vectors poised
and registered there in fleet equilibrium. In a nutshell, this seems to have been the way Hugh Kenner has
conceived the task of explicating Pound.(47)

It is a part of our program here to demonstrate
that a design can be discerned in Pound's so-called
"Paradise" Cantos, as well as latent in his work
overall. Yet no single image of Pound's "Paradise"
would be adequate to it. Nor could any one description or explanation ever be definitive. This is in
great part the point, and precisely what we have to
learn from Pound. The various frequencies are, as
Fuller would say, interaccommodative. Each "shows
through" the other; they neither appear independent-
ly nor ever wholly disappear. To coin a phrase,
the multivalent frequencies of Pound's "Paradiso"
transpear through one another, leaving the reader
the impression of a battery of lenses brought to
bear on various foci in various combinations.

In order to render these reflections somewhat
more concrete, it will be necessary for us to examine as it were a "cross-section" of the later
Cantos. In a sense, all the "strata" of the poem
can be seen if one looks hard enough and long
enough -- not only at, but through -- any one of the
myriad foci of attention(48) Pound provides. Our
test case will be the Dante material which surfaces
so abundantly in these later Cantos. We could perhaps more easily have chosen the Odyssean motifs and
followed Pound's personal periplus in that direction,
as others have done eloquently. But, as J. Wilhelm
has pointed out, "Perhaps the most important of the
cohering voices is that of Dante Alighieri."(49)

What we should like to effect by schematizing
the Dante material will be, in a manner of speaking,
a geometrical proof for at least one sort of coherence in Pound's "Paradiso." This can be done
minimally. It can perhaps only be done minimally.
It is not even necessary to go about establishing
the fact that there is a continuous string of references to Dante's Paradiso in the later Cantos.
They are well known.(50) What is more interesting
are the "nodes" we have been discussing, the places
where "planes intersect," where the Dante continuum
meets other referential continua, other "subject-
rhyme" schemes.(51) By simply registering several
such "nodes" or "islands of compression," we should

be able to triangulate a rough map by which the reader may attempt to navigate the "nonsimultaneous ocean of tension" that is <u>The Cantos</u>.

Counterpoint;
Pound On Harmony

Excerpts from Pound's Antheil, or the Treatise on
Harmony.*

Chapter One

I

    "What, mon élève, is the element grossly ommitted
from all treatises on harmony...?
    at this point the élève looks up brightly...
                                  "except the
treatise now being composed" ...? the élève continues
to regard me brightly... and blankly. No answer is
offered me.

    The answer, mon élève, is:

        The element most grossly ommited from
    treatises on harmony up to the present is the ele-
    ment of time. The question of the time-interval
    that must elapse between one sound and another if
    the two sounds are to produce a pleasing consonance
    or an interesting relation, has been avoided.

        And yet the simplest consideration of
    the physics of the matter by almost the simplest mathe-
    matician, should lead to equations showing that

            A sound of any pitch, or any combination
    of such sounds, may be followed by a sound of any
    other pitch, or any combination of such sounds,
    providing the time-interval between them is properly
    gauged; and this is true for any series of sounds,
    chords or arpeggios.

                        (III)

        The early students of harmony were so
    accustomed to think of music as something with a
    strong lateral or horizontal motion that they never
    imagined any one, any one could be stupid enough to
    think of it as static; it never entered their heads
    that people would make music like steam ascending
    from a morass.
        They thought of music as travelling rhythm
    going through points or barriers of pitch and pitch-
    combinations.

107

They have this concept in their blood, as
the oriental has his raga and his tala. It simply
never occurred to them that people would start with
static harmony and stick in that stationary position.

*   *   *

Credo

I believe in an absolute rhythm. E.P.
1910 with explanations.**
In 1910 I was working with monolinear
rhythm but one had already an adumbration that the
bits of rhythm used in verse were capable of being
used in musical structure, even with other dimensions.
Treatises on harmony will give you all
sorts of recipes for getting from one chord to
another (this is more or less reduced to a few
simple mechanisms); they do not stop to enquire
whether the transit by these means is interesting,
or, in a given situation, expressive.
That is supposed to be a matter of creative
genius. It is.

V

Any series of chords can follow any other,
provided the right time-interval is discovered. The
interesting sequences are probably those that demand
very set and definite intervals.
That is probably all we have to say in
this chapter.

CHAPTER THREE

The former treatises on harmony dealt with
static harmony, they may have defined harmony as
"simultaneous melody" or they may have sought some
other definition, but they did not consider that
lateral motion, the horizontal motion, and the time-
interval between succeeding sounds must affect the
human ear, and not only the ear but the absolute
physics of the matter. The question of where one
wave-node meets another, or where it banks against
the course of another wave to strengthen or weaken
its action, must be considered.

NEXT SECTION

various inconvenient items which the bud should
consider before becoming too fixed in its opinions.

I

What applies to harmony, or the "perpen-
dicular" or simultaneous melody "microphonically,"
applies also to the melody, i.e. the succeeding
notes of a series, to the interceptions of counterpoint, to the statement and answer in the fugue.

There is nothing whatever in music but a
composition of frequencies, microphonic and macro-
phonic.

IV

Some people have a sense of absolute frequency, others of proportional frequency.

i.e. some recognize the number of vibrations of the note.

Others recognize only the proportion of
vibrations of a note to some other note (pitch)
already given.

This proportional sensitivity is called
having a musical ear.

V

And the fight between these two kinds of
auditives has been going on from the time of Aristotle
and Ptolemy to the present. Thank heaven.

That is to say one party (mine) says: You
can not transpose. That is to say you can transpose
till you are blue in the face, but the thing after
transposition is not the same, i.e. does not sound
the same as it did before.

VII

After Dolmetsch*** tunes a clavichord, he
has slightly to untune it. Why? That is to say,
the proportion of the different notes remains correct but each note is sounded on two strings, and

109

these must not be in absolute accord. He says the
waves "cut" each other and ruin the resonance.

One may either graph this by picturing two
sound waves, the crests of which mutually bump and
depress each other, or you may say that the nodes
need a certain width, they must meet, but they must
meet as if on the knife's back and not on the razor's edge.

These prolegomena are not intended as the
complete whifflepink to deaf musicians. They are a
statement of points that should be considered before
contradicting the author.

9 The Divine Diaphany;

Hymns & Spheres

"Points define a periphery."(1)

The reader is solicited to accept the following schema for what it is: a periplus(2), a seafarer's sketch of land sightings, a guide for the next pilgrim. It is intended to serve much the same purpose as 'The Argument' preceding each canto of Binyon's Commedia: orientation.(3) It is neither a substitute nor a simulacrum for the text. Some familiarity with The Pisan Cantos, the Rock-Drill section, Thrones and the Drafts & Fragments must be presupposed: you should read the poem. Pound's approach to his study of Dante in The Spirit of Romance might provide us the glimmer of an introduction to his own program:

THE COMMEDIA

The Commedia, as Dante has explained in his Epistle to Can Grande, is written in four senses: the literal, the allegorical, the anagogical, and the ethical. For this form of arcana we find the best parallel in the expressions of mathematics. Thus, when we are able to see that one general law governs such a series of equations (4) as $3X3 + 4X4 = 5X5$, or written more simply, $3^2 + 4^2 = 5^2$, $6^2 + 8^2 = 10^2$, $12^2 + 16^2 = 20^2$, etc., express the common relation $a^2 + b^2 = c^2$. When one has learned common and analytic geometry, one understands that this relation, $a^2 + b^2 = c^2$ exists between two sides of the right triangle and its hypotenuse, and that likewise in analytics for the points forming the circumference of any circle. Thus to the trained mathematician, the cryptic $a^2 + b^2 = c^2$ expresses:

1st.   A series of abstract numbers in a certain relation to each other.

2nd.   A relation between certain abstract numbers.

3rd.   The relative dimensions of a figure; in this case a triangle.

4th.   The idea or ideal of the circle.

Thus the Commedia is, in the literal sense, a description of Dante's vision of a journey through the realms inhabited by the spirits of men after

111

death; in a further sense it is the journey of
Dante's intelligence through the states of mind
wherein dwell all sorts and conditions of men
before death; beyond this, Dante or Dante's intelligence may come to mean "Everyman" or "Mankind,"
whereat his journey becomes a symbol of mankind's
struggle upward out of ignorance into the clear
light of philosophy. In the second sense I give
here, the journey is Dante's own mental and spiritual development. In a fourth sense, the Commedia
is an expression of the laws of eternal justice;
"il contrapasso," the counterpass, as Bertran
calls it (Inferno, XXIV), or the law of karma,
if we are to use an Oriental term.(5)

The First Sphere

St. Denys: Angels(6)   In St. Denys' Celestial Hierarchies, the order of intelligences actually begins with the rank closest to God; the angels are thus the ninth and bottommost rank. Pound, however, moves as Dante does -- from the Earth, through the sphere of fire (the war raging round him), into this first "Heaven," and thence upward, toward the light.

Dante: Heaven of the Moon, souls of those with broken vows, or vows imperfectly performed.(7)

Pound: The Pisan Cantos, especially LXXIX-LXXXIV.(8)

Pound had considerable reason to believe that The Pisan Cantos might be the final installment of his poem. Unlike Dante's first sphere, then, Pound's Pisan testament is not presented as the prelude to further Cantos, and no orderly sequence of ascent is anticipated. But Pound himself registers his own breakthrough into Il Paradiso in these pages, and subsequent criticism only corroborates the reader's sense that here an "ecstatic" element enters the poem more forcefully than ever before.

Moreover, whether intentional or not, the correspondences with Dante's Heaven of the Moon are quite striking. It has been said that in The Pisan Cantos, the moon presides. A lunatic girl from a neighboring village throws herself against the chain-link fence of the compound where the US Army holds Pound captive, and cries into the night: "Io son la luna," "I am the moon."(9) Pound rhymes this "sorella la luna" with Cunizza of Dante's third sphere. She is ever just over his shoulder: "O moon, my pin-up... my chronometer."

What happens at Pisa is one of the most astonishing events in the history of English literature. The sacred marriage of Heaven and Earth -- "Zeus lies in Ceres' bosom" -- is played out in the poet's tent: "Elysium, though it were in the halls of Hell."(10) And in this hell of the Detention Training Center, the great poet in Pound is called forth -- "Prepare to go on a journey"(11) -- and struggles to shed the mask of the wartime "commentator." Memory, skill, pride in craft, refinement of medium...

these disciplines sustain him beyond hope. And then:

> Yet ere the season died a'cold...
> I rose through the aureate sky...(12)

And, à propos of our topic:

> By no means an orderly Dantescan rising,
> but as the wind veers...
> as the wind veers and the raft is driven.
>   (13)

"By no means an orderly Dantescan rising"; any casual reader would agree. Note however that even in his variances from Dante, Pound bears Dante in mind. This in itself should be enough to establish a polarity, a tension, a dynamic in Pound's eyes between Dante's Paradiso and his own pilgrimage. The "winds" and the "raft" of course invoke Odysseus, so that in this translucent "node" we witness the Dantescan "points" (which eventually define their own periphery) intersecting "with clean edge" the Homeric continuum. As the path forks, we elect for the time being to trace the Dante track, still largely caelum incognitum. We have been forewarned that Pound's presentation will not follow a strictly linear sequence; it has its own ups and downs, so to speak. As Pound jocularly puts it in Canto LXXIV, echoing Baudelaire's famous comment on hashish:

> Le Paradis n'est pas artificiel,
> but spezzato apparently
> it exists only in fragments
> unexpected excellent sausage,
> the smell of mint, for example (14)

The Second Sphere

St. Denys: Archangels

Dante: Heaven of Mercury, souls of the ambitious.(15)

Pound: Cantos 85-89, and The Confucian Odes.(16)

"Our dynasty came in because of a great sensibility."(17) Section Rock-Drill, written from St.
Elizabeth's Hospital for the Criminally Insane...
Canto 85, a digest of gleanings from the Shu-ching,
the Confucian History Classic, sets the tone, and
enables the reader to see the same paradigms for
good government and humane culture surfacing in
American revolutionary history, Cantos 86-89.

The circuit is completed by reference to
Dante's second sphere: Justinian recounts his
achievements as Law-giver, and provides a complete
history of Roman civilization from the first settle-
ment of Trojans on the Italian peninsula (cf.
Aeniad) to the destruction of Jerusalem by the
Emperor Titus.(18)

Only a few astute critics seem to recognize the
depth to which Pound carried his translation of the
Confucian ethic into the Anglo-American cultural
matrix. As Pound's Confucian Odes(19), the full
text of the Shih-ching, or Book of Poems, is
translated as if English had these songs as its own
classics before Chaucer. Pound achieves this extraordinary effect by allowing to reverberate in his
seemingly homespun translation every major idiom of
English literary history.(20) It is an underestimated tour de force. Similarly, the Chinese Canto
85 acts as a sustained basso throughout the three
American Cantos that follow it.

The Third Sphere

St. Denys: Principalities

Dante: Heaven of Venus, lovers: Cunizza, Fulk,
Rahab the harlot -- no remorse over past amours.(21)

Pound: Cantos 90-93, the area Kenner has noted
as that of the greatest "syncretic exaltation" in
the poem.(22)

"UBI AMOR IBI OCULUS EST"(23), "Where love is,
there the eye is" -- Richard of St. Victor speaking,
inverting Dante's relation of vision first, then
love consequent upon it (Paradiso, XXVIII, 109-14).
And in the sphere of Venus, so it is... Nowhere in
the poem is the Goddess more palpable than in these
three Cantos. Nowhere does he invoke and sustain
her presence more powerfully:

That the body of light come forth
            from the body of fire
And that your eyes come to the surface
            from the deep wherein they were sunken,
Reina -- for 300 years,
            and now sunken
That your eyes come forth from their caves...
                                                (24)

                    *

The Princess Ra-Set(25) has climbed
            to the great knees of stone,
She enters protection,
            the great cloud is about her,
She has entered the protection of crystal
                    convien che si mova
                    la mente, amando
                                    XXVI,34(26)
Light & the flowing crystal
            never gin in cut glass had such clarity

                    *

Gods moving in crystal
            ichor(27), amor(28)

        *   *   *

116

The Fourth Sphere

St. Denys: Powers

Dante: Heaven of the Sun, theologians: Thomas, Solomon, Denys, Boethius, Sigier, Richard.(29)

Pound: Cantos 94, 95. (30)

"Let the light pour..."(31) These two Cantos bring to focus the sun's light, filling heaven with its tensile radiance. All the threads and strands of light are gathered -- "to build light, said Ocellus"(32) -- until they become a stream, a river of light:

> So that walking here under the larches of Paradise
> the stream was exceedingly clear
> & almost level its margin
> "was thrown in my way a touch-stone..."(33)

As did Dante, Pound here assembles his own litany of theologians. Among the assembly are Kung, Mencius, Richard of St. Victor, Anselm, Dante himself, John Adams (who proved a formidable student of theology in the Adams/Jefferson correspondence), Hilary, St. Denys (or the pseudo-Dionysus; Pound exploits the pun on "Dionysus"), and above all, Apollonius of Tyana.

The importance of Philostratus' Life of Apollonius of Tyana(34) for this section of The Cantos has been somewhat neglected to date.(35) This Apollonius worships the sun. He travels from Greece to Egypt, through Babylonia to India, and finally returns to Greece, conversing with all manner of kings and sages along the way. He is also reputed to have understood the language of the birds. Wherever he finds bloodshed on the altar, he gently but firmly "rectifies" the rites and institutes bloodless sacrifice. Apollonius is numbered among the most illustrious disciples of Pythagoras (although it is another Apollonius(36) who is known for his geometry), and was at one time considered a "competitor" of Christ in the Mediterranean imagination.

Apollonius' conversations with the Indian brahmin Iarchus especially fascinated Pound. For example, he draws the following two lines --

117

and that the universe is alive

ἐρωτά ἴσχει   (37)

from a passage in Philostratus' Book III, Chapter
XXXIV, which to my knowledge has not been noted in
the Pound literature, and which bears strikingly
upon our presentation. The discussion begins with
the elements, and very quickly leads to the whole:

Apollonius again asked which was the first
of the elements, and Iarchus answered: "All
are simultaneous, for a living creature is not
born bit by bit." "Am I," said Apollonius, "to
regard the universe as a living creature?"
"Yes," said the other, "if you have a sound
knowledge of it, for it engenders all living
things." "Shall I then," said Apollonius,
"call the universe female, or of both the male
and the opposite gender?" "Of both genders,"
said the other, "for by commerce with itself it
fulfills the role of both mother and father in
bringing forth living creatures; and it is
possessed by a love for itself more intense
than any separate being has for its fellow, a
passion which knits it together into
harmony."(38)

*   *   *

The Fifth Sphere

St. Denys: Virtues

Dante: Heaven of Mars, warriors and martyrs for the faith. Dante learns of his banishment from Florence.(39)

Pound: Cantos 96-98. (40)

"The temple is holy because it is not for sale."(41) Back on the theme of money again, working from new material (Del Mar), Pound produces in this first group of Thrones a lexicographical puzzleworks, and perhaps the least scrutable of the later Cantos. One has the impression Stock may be at least half right about this section; the material does not seem to have been thoroughly digested. Further, the theme of money continues to so infuriate Pound that the poetry is somewhat knotted up, as if written with clenched fist.

But these three Cantos do contain as it were a "checklist of the good guys," recalling Dante's warriors and martyrs for the faith, e.g.: "Melik & Edwards struck coins-with-a-sword/ or the sword of the Prophet." (42)

For the reader unfamiliar with Del Mar's multi-volume overview of economic history, these three may remain the most opaque Cantos of all.(43) But the overriding point could not be more clear:

The temple ▟▟▙ is holy
because it is not for sale. (44)

*   *   *

119

The Sixth Sphere

St. Denys: Dominations

Dante: Heaven of Jupiter, "that temperate star."
Souls conspicuous for justice. The "Eagle"
speaks.(45)

Pound: Cantos 99-105. Canto 99 is the
heart(46), 100-105 mainly amplifications, ramifications, socio-economic sidelights.

"Giustizia." Iong Cheng's edict(47): "Food is
the root, feed the people."(48) The Great Balance
outspread in perfect harmony: "Completeness, focus,
or ruin"(49). "Greed" replaces "usury" in Pound's
demonology.(50) There is a recording available of
Pound reading Canto 99(51); the voice is that of the
Elder instructing the tribe on the rites by virtue
of which they may dwell on Earth and under Heaven as
humane beings. The Balance is there in nature,
mirrored in the actions of men, and illuminated "by
the silk cords of the sunlight/ Chords of the sunlight."(52) The text speaks as if carved in gra-
nite:

Heaven, man, earth, our law as written
                    not outside their natural colour(53)
                    *

...believed in the peoples,
Different each, different customs
                    but one root in the equities,
One in acumen,
                    with the sun (chih)
                                        under it all
                    & faith with the word
Hills and streams colour the air,
                    vigour, tranquility,
                                        not one set of rules(54)
                                        *

Confucians observe the weather,
                    hear thunder
                    seek to include... (55)
                    *

The fu jen receives heaven, earth, middle
                    and grows. (56)

            *   *   *

The Seventh Sphere

St. Denys: Thrones, perfection. (57)

Dante: Heaven of Saturn, souls of the con-
templatives. Beatrice's beauty becomes almost un-
bearable. Peter Damian and St. Benedict discourse
on the decadence of the Church. (58)

Pound: Cantos 106-109. (59)

"So slow is the rose to open... a match flares
in the eye's hearth, then darkness." (60)

Canto 106 is the nub of it; the final full
apparition of the Goddess:

between the two pine trees, not Circe
but Circe was like that
coming from the house of smoothe stone
"not know which god"
nor could enter her eyes by probing
the light blazed behind her
nor was this from sunset.(61)

"God's eye art'ou"(62), he exclaims at the last.
And, indeed, why is it one cannot "enter her eyes"?
Cunizza, in Dante's third sphere, gave the clue:
Thrones are mirrors. (63) So are Beatrice's eyes.

The vision of the Goddess fades and is followed
by a long stretch of critiques, not unlike Peter
Damian's discourse, and far too protracted to trace
here; the last two lines are a double Dante chord.(64)
Note that Pound nowhere uses much of Dante's material;
only the principle of organization remains, a knot
slipped from one sort of rope to another.(65)

*   *   *

121

The Fixed Stars

St. Denys: Cherubim, illumination.

Dante: The Fixed Stars, located "beyond the spheres"; all the other planets visible. Dante is interrogated on Faith, Hope and Love. Vision of the Virgin. (66)

Pound: Drafts & Fragments (67)

Pound in his way also interrogates himself on the topics of faith, hope and love. On the final point, he finds himself wanting: "Charity I have had sometimes, I cannot make it flow through." (68) It seems likely that by convicting himself of not having loved enough, Pound disqualifies himself from the final vision of the Rose, thus likening himself finally to Icarus: "So high toward the sun and then falling." (69) The vision of the Virgin is however intact, if somewhat soiled:

> The vision of the Madonna
> above the cigar butts
> and over the portal (70)

This final segment of the poem nonetheless includes some of the most beautiful and haunting lines Pound ever penned. Remember that these are fragments of light -- scintilla -- and the conjunction with Dante's Fixed Stars is clear enough. References abound to the spheres already passed through, and the spirits encountered there: "these had thrones, and in my mind were still, uncontending..." (71) The voice seems to be hushing itself, almost whispering... as Pound at this time in his life entered into several years of public silence, during where eerie period many people (including, in my own experience, two university Professors of English Literature) supposed him dead.

In an uncanny way, the "catholicity" of these final Cantos is stunning. These "fragments" CONTAIN the whole work, "as the thought of the tree is in the seed." They span and comprehend and celebrate 70 years of acute awareness. They are Pound's final flowering; a pale, autumnal blossom:

> From time's wreckage shored,
> these fragments shored against ruin.(72)
> *   *   *

122

Primum Mobile

St. Denys: Seraphim, purification

Dante: Primum Mobile, the first mover and ninth
(nonspherical) heaven, from which the entire angelic
hierarchy receives its impulse. The divine essence
is revealed to Dante as a single point of intensely
shining light. (73)

Pound: Canto CXX. (74)

CXX

I have tried to write Paradise

Do not move
   Let the wind speak
            that is paradise.

Let the Gods forgive what I
            have made

Let those I love try to forgive
            what I have made.(75)

   This Canto is the only audible coda to Pound's
turn to silence. It contains an apparent repudia-
tion of the attempt to speak the unspeakable. This
is the "single point" (76) with which Pound leaves
his poem, and us. It is worthy, in its candor and
poignancy, of comparison with Chaucer's "retraction"
at the end of The Canterbury Tales (77), and Shake-
speare/Prospero's at the end of that magician's
final play, The Tempest. (78)

        *   *   *

The Rose

St. Denys: The Thearchy, the Trinity, about which he says nothing, probably because there is nothing to say. (79)

Dante: The Sempiternal Rose, the Empyrean, the river of light. Dante ends his poem with a prayer that he might through his verse convey some inkling of the mystery of the Trinity. (80)

Pound: Here we are stopped short. All the final stages -- the Rose, the Empyrean, etc. -- are missing.

Pound's Paradiso does not seem to go beyond the Primum Mobile, from which all the other heavens and their respective intelligences are revealed. Yet Pound also registers something of the trinitarian mystery.

In Pound, the first three spheres seem to present the dominant archetype of Love, culminating the third heaven, Cantos 90-93. The second triad bodies forth Justice in the human world, and reaches its crescendo in Canto 99. Except for a few irritating distractions and digressions, the final stages are sheer Beauty(81), a transparency through which the other spheres are more "visible"(82) than ever before. At this point there is a sorrow deep in Pound, plus perhaps an element of remorse, that is not evident in Dante. All the heavens interpenetrate in the final Fragments, and then all are thrown into stark relief by the "renunciation" of Canto CXX. The upshot of this final gesture is perhaps also conveyed by the epitaph the troubador Arnaut Daniel composed for himself: "I am Arnaut, who loved the wind, and chased the hare with the ox."(83)

In a similar vein, we ought to note a few enigmatic lines Pound rendered at the end of his life from the Fenollosa notes -- a passage, as Kenner remarks, he would not have bothered with during his early Cathay translations.(84) It concerns... personified constellations of stars, the "drawing-ox-star" never quite catching up with the "weaving-girl-star"; and she (perhaps weaving and unweaving as Penelope did while awaiting Odysseus' return) making "no pattern today..." Kenner prints two versions of this little poem:

```
                She weaves and ends no pattern to day
                                Milky Way girl
            and the heavy ox pulls and pulls
            to the end of the day no pattern
            Via lactea clear and shallow
            far from each other
                    one wide river to cross.
```

Or, in even sharper focus:

```
            By the river of stars, its brightness
                    the ox-herd far from star-girl
            her white hand on the shuttle
                    and at day's end no pattern yet made

            a rain of tears for their distance
                    tho the river is clear and shallow
                    they cannot cross it;

            nor their pulse beat, come into words.(85)
```

"That love is the 'form' of philosophy," Pound
wrote in Canto 93, "is its shape (è forma di
Filosofia)." (86)

Need more be said?

Paradise is when it ceases to be a problem.

*   *   *

If the preceding schema establishes nothing else, it suffices that one periplus, one "subject-rhyme" in the round, one "horizon" of the poem's intelligibility has been outlined. We have chosen to follow the Dantescan "great circle route" through the later Cantos. Others, as noted, have followed the Odyssean return or the Confucian process, both of which motifs are vigorously alive in the post-Pisan Cantos. (87)

For our purposes, one need not prove that more than one or two such interpenetrating patterns are intact -- the point is made, and its periphery defined. In a tensional system configured as are the later Cantos(88), no such "referential continuum" could stave off collapse if most of the others were not also intact.(89)

This property of tensegrity systems can be graphically demonstrated, and we shall do so in the Illustrations to follow. (90)

Illustrations: The Image As Word

a/ Periplum: Paradiso;
Ezra Pound Speaking

Luminous Details

The artist selects the luminous detail
and presents it. He does not comment.
These facts are hard to find. They
are swift and easy of transmission. (1)

Mental Voltage

Grosseteste on Light may or may not be
scientific but at least his mind gives us a
structure. He throws onto our spectrum a
beauty comparable to a work by Max Ernst. The
mind making forms can verbally transmit them
when the mental voltage is high enough. It is
not absolutely necessary that the imagination
be registered either by sound or on painted
canvas. (2)

The Matter of Dante's Paradiso

We appear to have lost the radiant world
where one thought cuts through another with
clean edge, a world of moving energies (mezzo
oschuro rade, risplende in se perpetuale
effecto...), magnetisms that take form, that
border on the visible, the matter of Dante's
Paradiso, the glass under water, the form that
seems a form seen in a mirror...

A medieval natural philosopher would find
this modern world full of enchantments, not
only the light in the electric bulb, but the
thought of the current hidden in air and in
wire would give him a mind full of forms...
The medieval philosopher would probably have
been unable to think of the electric world and
not think of it as a world of forms. Perhaps
algebra has queered our geometry. (3)

The Serious Artist

We might come to believe that the thing
that matters in art is a sort of energy, something more or less like electricity or radioac-

tivity, a force transfusing, welding and unifying. A force rather like water when it
spurts up through very bright sand and sets it
in swift motion. You may make what image you
like. (4)

Lords Over Fact

The statements of analytic geometry are
"lords" over fact. They are the thrones and
dominations that rule over form and recurrence.
And in like manner are great works of art lords
over fact, over race-long recurrent moods, and
over tomorrow. (5)

The Case of the Ovoid

I do not know by what metaphorical paraphrase I am to convey the relation of these
ovoids to Brancusi's other sculpture. As an
interim label, one might consider them as
master-keys to the world of form -- not "his"
world of form, but as much as he has found of
"the" world of form. They contain or imply, or
should, the triangle and the circle.

In the case of the ovoid, I take it
Brancusi is meditating on pure form free from
all terrestrial gravitation; form as free in
its own life as the form of the analytic geo-
meters; and the measure of his success in this
experiment (unfinished and probably unfinish-
able) is that from some angles at least the
ovoid does come to life and appear ready to
levitate.

Crystal-gazing?? No. Admitting the possibility of self-hypnosis by means of highly
polished brass surfaces, the polish, from the
sculptural point of view, results merely from a
desire for greater precision of the form; it is
also a transient glory. But the contemplation
of form or of formal-beauty leading into the
infinite must be dissociated from the dazzle of
crystal; there is a sort of relation, but there
is the more important divergence; with the
crystal it is a hypnosis or a contemplative
fixation of thought, or an excitement of the
"sub-conscious" or unconscious (whatever the
devil they may be), and with the ideal form in
marble it is an approach to the infinite by

<u>form</u>, by precisely the highest possible degree
of consciousness of formal perfection; as free
of accident as any of the philosophical demands
of a "Paradiso" can make it.

This is not a suggestion that all sculpture should end in the making of abstract
ovoids; indeed no one but a genius wholly cen-
tered in his art, and more or less "oriental"
could endure the strain of such effort. (6)

b/ Geomancy

In his Gaudier-Brzeska, Pound stresses analytic geometry as an "idiom" in which "one is able actually to create."(7)   Such a notion stands at rather a far remove from conventional applications of the Cartesian analytic.   Once Pound embarks on The Cantos, even more radical divergences appear.   The "circle free of space and time limits... universal, existing in perfection"(8) opens out into the "spheres within spheres" of the medieval light philosophers.   And the coordinate system Pound eventually develops in The Cantos emphatically includes the dimension of time, as the two-dimensional Cartesian geometry does not.(9)   There is however a geometry adequate to this vision.   In the same year that Pound, echoing Gaudier, was calling for "organic forms in sculpture," R. Buckminster Fuller was busy discovering what he came to call "Nature's coordinate system":

> In 1917, I found myself asserting that I didn't think nature had a department of chemistry, a department of mathematics, a department of physics, and a department of biology and had to have meetings of department heads in order to decide what to do when you drop your stone in the water.   Universe, i.e. nature, obviously knows just what to do, and everything seemed beautifully coordinate.   The lily pads did just what they should do, and the fish did just what they should do.   Everything went sublimely, smoothly.
>
> So I thought that nature probably had one coordinate system and probably one most economical arithmetical and geometric system with which to interaccount all transactions and transformations.
>
> And I thought also that it was preposterous when I was told that real models are not employed in advanced science, because science was able to deal with nature by use of completely unmodelable mathematical abstractions. I could not credit that universe suddenly went abstract at some micro-level of investigation, wherefore you had to deal entirely with abstract-formula, unmodelable mathematics... I thought then that if we could find nature's own coordinate system we would understand the models and would be able to develop much higher explora-

tory and application capability. I felt that
if we ever found nature's coordinate system, it
would be very simple and always rational. (10)

Perhaps this passage helps clarify why Pound
saw fit, in 1971, to break his self-imposed silence
in order to hail Buckminster Fuller as:

> friend of the universe
> liberator
> bringer of happiness (11)

Since Fuller apparently did find such a coordinate
system, and spent the next 50 years articulating it,
we might also have a clue as to why Hugh Kenner,
surely the most revered and authoritative Pound
critic, has devoted two books in recent years to
Fuller: Bucky, A Guided Tour of Buckminster Fuller,
probably the best available introduction, and Geodesic Math, a more technical follow-up.(12) In this
latter work, Kenner makes it possible for the architect or designer or student of geodesic math to gen-
erate complex multi-frequency structures -- ellipses,
egg-shapes and so on. Our own approach in these
Illustrations is through some of the very simplest
such figures, but the spectrum of form values is
much the same as that with which Kenner, and of
course Bucky himself, is working.

A presentation of certain primary patterns in
this "geometry of organic forms" follows. A couple
of points should be mentioned beforehand, since what
we are dealing with is more an exploratory probe than
a finished product. Fuller calls his synergetics
"the geometry of thinking," which should cue us early
on that the emphasis here is on a qualitative
geometry, a geometry of qualities, values; in short,
a geomancy, if the archaism is permissible. (13)

Now the first principle of synergetics, the very
definition of syn-ergy that Fuller prefers, runs as
follows: "Behavior of whole systems unpredictable
from their components, or from any sub-assembly of
their components."(14) Fuller then adds to this a
corollary: Knowing the behavior of the whole, and
the behavior of some of the parts, one may be able to
predict the behavior and disposition of unknown
parts.(15) Precisely this principle has allowed us
access to the larger patterns of coherence in Ezra
Pound's poetic enterprise. In sum, the geomancer
divines his truths from consideration of whole

131

systems(16), much as the Tantrist utilizes the
traditional <u>yantra</u> in his own contemplation of the
real.

ŚRĪ YANTRA

c/ Nonlinear Patterns of Coherence

WHOLES are geodesic sculptures Mr. John Blackman and I have derived from specifications first published in R.B. Fuller's Synergetics (1975). After developing the figures in clear and reflective media, we showed them to Fuller, who pronounced them "Beautifully done," and gave us his blessing to christen the spectrum of models WHOLES (pun intended). To distinguish WHOLES from geodesics and tensegrity figures, WHOLES are great circle models. In the clear material, this feature is especially prominent; it is a dimension of Fuller's geometry (what happens at the center?!) not previously modeled effectively. Since tension is invisible, it occured to us that the only way to render the tensional continuity of such a system visible would be to construct it out of as clear a material as possible. Fuller's collaborator E.J. Applewhite has written that the results are "the most beautiful models of the foldable geometries that I have ever seen." (17) Line drawings provide a more exact and informative rendering of WHOLES than do photographs. Mr. Thomas Parker has provided the following drawings of three such transparent great circle models: 1) spherical vector equilibrium, 2) spherical icosidodecahedron, and 3) spherical rhombic dodecahedron.

A suggestion: Check Fuller's Synergetics for the specifications and unfold a few WHOLES for yourself.(18) There is no substitute for experience. Following Pound:

> An image, in our sense, is real because we know it directly. If it have an age-old traditional meaning this may serve as proof to the professional student of symbology that we have stood in the deathless light, or that we have walked in some arbour of his traditional paradiso, but that is not our affair. It is our affair to render the image as we have perceived or conceived it.

> Browning's "Sordello" is one of the finest masks ever presented. Dante's "Paradiso" is the most wonderful image. By that I do not mean that it is a perseveringly imagistic performance. The permanent part is Imagisme, the rest, the discourses with the calendar of saints and the discussions about the nature of the moon, are philology. The form of sphere

133

above sphere, the varying reaches of light, the
minutiae of pearls upon foreheads, all these
are parts of the Image. The image is the
poet's pigment... (19)

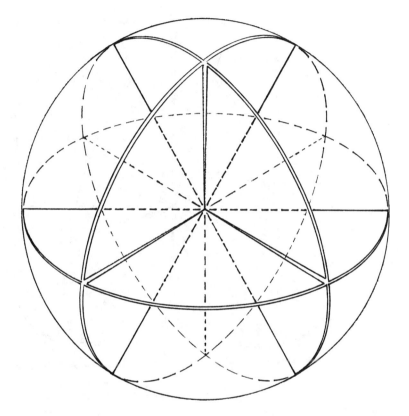

SPHERICAL VECTOR EQUILIBRIUM

135

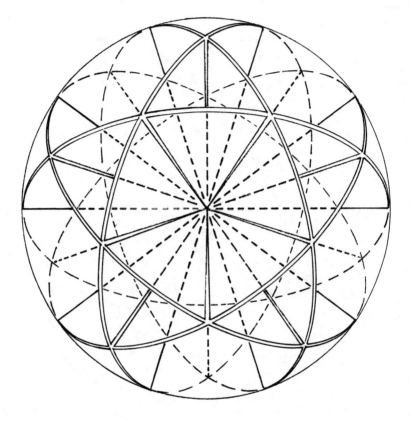

SPHERICAL ICOSIDODECAHEDRON

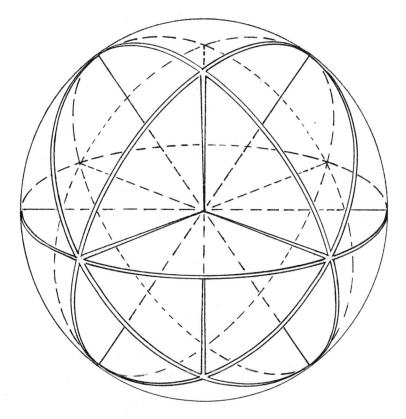

SPHERICAL RHOMBIC DODECAHEDRON

137

III <u>The Poet As Psychopomp</u>

"By this door have I entered the hill.
Falleth,
Adonis falleth.
Fruit cometh after."(1)

Several matters still require attention. First of all, there is this question of the "better place." What and where is it? We began our investigation with the problematic of the proper end of Man. Has Ezra Pound's work given us any clue as to how this problematic might be resolved?

Indeed, we have had many clues. The main direction of inquiry we have opened up is that toward a resolution of the so-called subject/object dichotomy. Once these two "poles" or "shores" of the entire reality are reified or substantivized -- viz., when there is supposed to be one "thing" over here called Man, and another "thing" over there called World, Matter or Cosmos -- then these two "things" can never be reconciled. We have however seen that it is plausible to understand subject and object as limit cases of the verbal unity which generates and sustains them. In this way, the common integrity of Man and Cosmos is not ruptured, nor is the vital and healthy tension between these "poles" dissipated.

It is possible to glimpse Ezra Pound shifting, over a span of years, from a (subjective) idealized paradise to a more (objective) realistic utopian vision, and then back again. He began with the classicist's devotion to a "golden age" which he felt might be recaptured if only he could awaken enough contemporary literati and illuminati to the task. World War I blasted this hope, and the Mauberley sequence registers Pound taking another tack.(2) He never really loses his nostalgia for this "golden age," but increasingly he pins his hopes for a Renaissance on socio-political tactics and economic reform.

Accordingly, he poured much of his energy into a study of government and governments which would lead him in little over a decade to the "totalitarian" ("of or pertaining to the whole," in Pound's unusual understanding of the term "totalitarian") ideal as it began to burgeon in his beloved Italy. It has been said that Pound's interest in Italian fascism (he never joined anything) was spurred mainly by the innovative economic policies of Mussolini's finance minister, presumably the famous fellow who got the trains running on time... Be this as it may, a second World War would soon enough pull the rug out from Pound's utopian fancies.

141

Meanwhile, in his own affairs, Pound's early success as a poet in London and Paris had gradually undermined itself. His very prominence in the world of letters gave him the temerity to embark on an unfinished magnum opus that was less and less comprehensible to his former adherents, or to the reading public at large. By the mid-thirties, Pound was already isolated in Italy, scornful, alienated, angry at a world he felt was inevitably courting war after war, and embittered that nobody would listen to him. His sense of balance and proportion seemed to desert him; he struck out blindly and caustically. Even so, he did little damage except to himself. His effect on the politics of his day was certainly negligible. If he had not allowed the hideous anti-semitism of his time to infect his public pronouncements like a creeping cancer, he might more easily have been forgiven his other wartime excesses. His personal position cannot quite be aligned with either side in the conflict; it can be said that Pound was vehemently opposed to World War II.

After the war, his early success had come full circle and he found himself branded not only a traitor to his country (while he considered himself a patriot), but a madman as well (a verdict no jury in its right mind would uphold today). Ironically, Pound's purported insanity may very well have saved him from being hung for his purported treasons. His personal success had transformed itself into his personal tragedy with all the inexorability of a Greek drama, complete with "tragic flaw."

So -- where take refuge? In Pisa and thereafter, Pound sought what can fairly be termed an ideal "state of mind," more perdurable than utopian schemes or individual success stories. He would write from Pisa: "4 times was the city rebuilded/ now in the mind indestructible" (3), and these more subjective "states of mind" -- love chief among them -- would lead him to some of the highest raptures of his Paradiso, as we have seen.

Yet even here, as Pound passed through his seventh and into his eighth decade, the "better place" he sought slowly eroded. He began to have trouble concentrating, let alone aligning and attuning the myriad details and seeming loose ends of his vast poem. His "state of mind" became one of exasperation, self-recrimination and not inconsider-

142

able suffering. Age, too, was catching up with him:
"... the plain fact is that my head just doesn't
WORK. Stretches when it just doesn't work."(4) Is
Pound at the end of his long life only the shadow of
his former self?   Did he once hold the vision and
then squander it? As Professor Eloise Hay has rightly inquired, "Wasn't his pilgrimage a failure except
insofar as he stuck to his original insight... of a
'heavenly light' to be found in the 'natural object'?"(5)   Did he make no progress at all in the
latter 50 years of his life?

     Noel Stock comes more or less directly to such a
conclusion at the end of his Pound biography.(6)
Indeed, there is something like a critical consensus
(excluding Davie, Kenner, Pearlman, Hesse and other
Poundians we have cited) on this point.   Undeniably,
such a view provides a certain leverage on Pound's
later work.   Pound becomes a formative influence on
Anglo-American poetry in the early 20th century, and
from then on merely a backslider and a miscreant
meddling where he had no business anyway.   Literary
criticism may be able to content itself with such a
viewpoint; it is happy to circumscribe the difficult
case of Ezra Pound.   But such a view falls short of
encompassing not only what Pound did and said during
the second half of his active life (to the increasing
consternation of many readers, no doubt), but also
what he meant to say and intended to do throughout.
Such an arbitrarily truncated criticism can hardly
serve us as an adequate understanding of Pound's
poetic odyssey.   It is as if the critics shook their
knowing heads, clucked their tongues in unison, and
prudently concluded Odysseus would have been better
off had he never left the safety of Ithaca.

     In the terms we have taken the liberty to sug-
gest, Pound spent much of the rest of his life ex-
hausting the gamut of expectations and projections
of the ultimate end of Man.   "It is difficult to
write a paradiso when all the superficial indications are that you ought to write an apocalypse."
He did not die a contented man (1972).   He had not
reached a single one of the "goals" he had set
himself. And yet --

     As we have experienced for ourselves, Pound's
life and work open the door to a new and more radical
reflection on contemporary Man's paths to such goals.
In a sense, Pound's life came to a pass where he was
obliged to "Pound," at least the public persona,

143

behind him. He himself -- given the strict terms his
enormous ego set up for itself -- was a failure in
his own eyes. But a failure of a very special variety. Something in him had come to an understanding
with the entire reality, just as some passages in his
work will live forever. Something in him had made
the important discovery that the metaphysical dimension to human life -- the "Paradise," the apotheosis
so ardently sought -- is neither an addition to reality nor some sort of crutch lying outside the human
predicament. The clearest formulation of this understanding is to be found in his Chinese studies. Here
Heaven is the sheer relativity of Man and Earth,
subject and object, inner and outer: their "belonging
together." Pound's poetic quest began when he meta-
phorically allowed himself to become a tree -- "and
many a new thing understood."(7) It ends with a "a
blown husk that is finished/ but the light sings
eternal."(8)

These threads are of course woven into the material comprising Part II of this study, but now we
should pause to consider the upshot. To paraphrase
Pound's paraphrase of Confucius: "What you depart
from is not your path." Granting the integrity of
the entire reality, as Pound does, it can thus be
declared that ALL human "paths to the goal" are
viable, providing only that they are persevered in,
really followed up, lived out, pursued to their
ultimate term.(9) There are no straight lines in
all universe, only great-circle pathways of energy
in constant transaction and transformation. Contemporary Man is in a splendid position; he has run out
of escape routes. Perhaps now it is possible for us
to encounter the whole cloth of reality; its coherence, its beauty, and its mystery. Perhaps we may
come, as Pound did, to celebrate that mystery...

Here the question of style -- customarily considered merely a means to an end -- becomes crucial,
and our encounter with Ezra Pound has prepared us to
re-evaluate the conventional approach to style
through grammar and prosody. Important as these
aesthetic issues are within the purview of literary
criticism, there is a fundamental human concern here
which is too often and too easily overlooked.

The world stylus has fallen so far into cliché
and banality that it has come to mean fashion and
affectation. We too easily assume that "style" is
supererogatory, a little "polish" added on to the sub-

stance of what we do, say, think and are. But the original intuition cuts much deeper, as the etymology of the word indicates. The stylus is originally the point; and in its deepest sense the style is always the life-style, the "point" of one's life, which is that way that life is lived. Your style is the way that you are; nothing less, nothing more. Following the criteria we have unearthed in Pound's work, the optimum life-style would be the most transparent one. Your style is the way that you live your life -- i.e., by transforming it, by turning yourself into yourself. It is not an afterthought or an affectation; on the contrary, it is the very freedom at the core of being human. The goal of authentic life and the way to it are in this sense the same: The style is the point. And so? The quest continues. The unfinished character of the human pilgrimage -- ever suspended between Earth and Heaven -- is also its non-finite, infinite dimension.

During the course of this study, we have attempted to understand the poetic enterprise as a human horizon of meaning; for this reason we saw fit to present Ezra Pound's work over against the backdrop of the three worlds -- cosmic, human and divine, following our terminology -- and in terms of the deeply human question of the proper end of Man. As one result, we have begun to discern how the poet speaks to the human predicament. Homo viator: We are all pilgrims here -- on Earth, under Heaven -- however greatly our paths may diverge in other ways. What more basic issue concerns and confronts us at every turn?

And yet we have found that the poet lives this question of style, or rather life-style, in an altogether curious way. The "measure-taking" that the poet accomplishes cannot be reduced to prosody only. To be sure, every poet has his or her own "measure," a characteristic diction, one prosodic option among a range of conventional metric "styles." It is much more than that, of course. Pound's characteristic "signature," as Kenner has pointed out, is a peculiar spondee terminating the line, e.g.:

If a man have not order withín hím,

He cannot spread order abóut hím. (10)

145

Behind this personal "breathing pattern" that is the voice of Ezra Pound, we have also glimpsed the poet taking that other, deeper measure -- spanning Earth and Heaven, Cosmos and Theos -- by which the free-space for humane civilization first opens up and is preserved in the poem. Martin Heidegger has insisted that this poetic measure-taking must be considered the most primordial stratum of human dwelling, the "measure for all measuring," the foundational act on which will be based all subsequent building, dwelling and thinking. (11)

By now it should be clear how and to what extent this is true. Our study of Ezra Pound's poetic development -- commencing with a literary re-evaluation of metaphor and image, unfolding into an ethical vision grounded in the Confucian "rectification of terms," and culminating in a fitful celebration of the metaphysical integrity of the entire reality -- our study attests that that larger measure has indeed been gauged anew in Pound's work. A further horizon of "the poetic" has come to light. Poiesis can no longer mean for us just homo faber "making" one artifact or another; by virtue of Pound's work we are enabled to envision poetry as way-making... the forging of the link, the bridge, the path "wide as a hair"(12) leading from the given human predicament to the realization of human life in its plenitude. The poet is the pathfinder...

The poet in our day has no choice but to gauge this more encompassing measure within the global context of the encounter of cultures. It is no coincidence that the possibility for planetary human community should today arise hand-in-hand with the possibility for planetary human suicide. Any mis-step could be catastrophic. The question of the proper end of Man has never been more urgent or acute than it now is for humankind as a whole. If the crisis is not faced with all its cross-cultural over- and under-tones, it is not faced at at all. Pound' example might teach us that the poet in our time must reanimate the spirit of his more provincial ancestor -- the shaman psychopompos, guide of souls -- and inscribe it on this global horizon, or else betray his calling. As Pound discerned, it is the cross-fertilization of living traditions which determines the shape of the "new word" for today, and for tomorrow.

146

In another sense, the quest to surmount the contemporary human impasse could not be a more personal one. The "better place" that concerns most of us most of the time is not the end of a quarrelsome species of wingless bipeds; it is your fate, and mine, and that of the next fellow that concern us. Since one obvious danger of cross-cultural and inter-disciplinary inquiry is that of superficial eclecticism, a study of the proper aim of the human pilgrimage must have reliable roots in lived human experience. It is hoped that the life and works of Ezra Pound have provided us a setting at once concrete enough and universal enough that neither the personal nor the traditional parameters of the question have been unduly neglected. If it does not speak to the reality of the human person, the "new word" does not speak at all. Moreover, Pound himself has encouraged us to grasp at least the rudiments of a common language between an "objective" science concerned with rhythms and patterns articulated in the natural world, and a "subjective" humanism concerned with language, ethics and right relations between people and peoples. The extremes meet -- and embrace. It is of the essence of the poetic way-making that it be also a healing, a making whole.

Our bridge between these outer and inner dimensions of Pound's _poiesis_ has been provided by the persistent theme of shamanic initiation. Thus we have been able to discern, stage by precarious stage, how the personal transformation of the shaman/poet comes to form the basis for world renewal. But initiation is only the beginning... Having once faced and overcome King Death, the self-healed healer begins to function as guide of souls for the human community at large. In this sense, wily Odysseus stands out as the exemplary shaman for the pre-Christian western tradition. Here it is crucial to recall that the medium of this renewal and recovery is precisely the shaman's song: Odysseus telling his tale in Phaecia. By means of the song, the healing cycle comes full circle. The song not only recapitulates and "re-members" the shaman's original journey and dismemberment in the underworld, it also "re-collects" all the scattered elements of the entire reality into an integrated ensemble of experience. The song gives the shaman wings: it is the ladder, the pole or staff, the tunnel or vortex, the bole of the cosmic tree: it is the vehicle, Odysseus' "craft," the axis mundi, the mediator, the passage between worlds. In so many words, the song (in our

case, Pound's <u>Cantos</u>) is not only the journey re-
told, but the <u>return</u> completed: <u>The song is the
way</u>...

But what is this "way" the poet has made?
What is the word for it? By what name shall we
know it? We have been able to examine close at
hand some of its "structure," as it were the
grammar of relations between Heaven, Earth and Man,
but have we really heard what this "word" has to
say to us? Not quite. Like the concentric
peelings of an onion, the word of the poet has
successively bared to us its metaphorical,
"imagistic," ritual, ethical and even geometrical
facets. And throughout this study, we have been at
pains to stress word and image, <u>logos</u> and <u>eidos</u>,
saying and showing, as twin facets of language.(13)
Hence our emphasis on the linguistic character of
the creative imagination, and the revelatory
character of the poetic word. To this point, then,
it all might be described as an essay to restore to
the word some of its cosmological and theological
rapports. But what is at the center of the onion?
Traditionally, the "word" concerning Man's progress
toward ultimate horizons is preeminently "the Word"
or message of salvation -- the Savior, the Promised
One who proclaims the Kingdom of Heaven, the long-
awaited Paradise.(14) Are we able to discover whether this "saving Word" may yet be reconstituted as
an orientation for human life?

Consider the case of Ezra Pound.

The ultimate success or failure of Pound's
poetic odyssey, including his projected "Paradiso,"
depends on the extent to which he has been able to:

a) take that larger measure between Earth
and Heaven within which human life defines and
articulates itself, and

b) communicate this "way" to his readers,
so that they might incorporate the vision into
their own lives.

Did he succeed? I would advance the following cautious thesis: Ezra Pound's paradise, latent throughout his poetic canon, amounts to the sheer <u>creative</u> <u>freedom</u> with which he allows diverse <u>cultural and</u> <u>linguistic</u> worlds to meet intelligibly in his work. I am suggesting that the redeeming virtue of Pound's work is precisely the much-maligned "poetic license" with which he relentlessly strives to "make it new." This creative freedom is nothing less than the "way" Pound has discovered... To the extent that he has been able to communicate the spark, the impulse, the motive power of that freedom to his readers, his poetic odyssey is a stirring success. To the extent that it remains only <u>his</u> "paradisiacal vision" (for which we may damn or <u>commend</u> him, small matter), his work falls short of its aim.

It would be fatuous merely to declare that Pound succeeded because he managed to communicate this "new measure" of creative freedom to succeeding generations of poets -- although he surely did so. It is more to the point that we see how Pound helped to create and sought to preserve a cultural milieu where certain sorts of poetry -- more innovative, perhaps, certainly more unusual than the conventional prosodic "outer limits" of free verse and blank verse -- forms that were not even thinkable before Pound, have flourished and become common practice since his time. Were we content to trace Pound's literary influence, one could easily make of him the "poet's poet" of 20th century Anglo-American letters.(15) Or one could almost as easily make the contrary case and contend that Pound's work failed because it has by and large been ignored except by a handful of poets and critics. But whatever the outcome, a purely literary evaluation would reach only halfway to our main question: How does Pound's work contribute to our understanding of the fundamental human predicament? It is thus our thesis here that Pound's poetic odyssey, including his "unfinished" <u>Paradiso</u>, opens up the dimension of creative <u>freedom within</u> which the human pilgrimage unfolds toward its fruition. The "proper end" of Man is ever a new beginning: <u>freedom</u>. But is this merely a poet's vision, or a <u>way of life</u> that we may recognize and eventually appropriate as our own? What does freedom mean to us?

Traditionally, and almost by definition, freedom is what every human being desires and aspires to; under one name or another -- deliverance, salvation,

release, fulfillment -- it has always been the pro-
mise most religions make to their believers. Each
of the paths to the "better place" examined earlier
were also in essence quests for freedom. Their
common failing was a willingness to settle for partial liberations.

Nowadays liberation is also the tempting pro-
mise served up by our secular "religions" (democracy,
marxism, nationalism, big business) to those they
wish to convert (or exploit). Even the most totalitarian regimes avow freedom -- from want, from
strife, even from oppression -- as their ultimate
aim and justification. Everywhere freedom is pro-
claimed the goal, meaning and purpose of human life.
But so often there is such a price to pay! You have
to join this or that, act in such and such a way,
think according to the party platform, and so on.
We might call this first variety of freedom, even
when espoused by religious institutions, political
freedom, implying by this mainly that it is a kind
of freedom which makes sense only within the political and economic framework of a given society. Ezra
Pound's predicament only makes painfully obvious the
intrinsic limitations of this species of freedom.

There are, further, certain cultural discrepan-
cies in the way people envision freedom.(16) We in
the west (very generally) tend to view freedom as
freedom to -- to do, say or think what we want,
where and with whom we please. These are the kinds
of freedom guaranteed by the Bill of Rights. In
certain eastern traditions with which we are becoming increasingly acquainted, Buddhism and Hinduism, for example, freedom is (and again, very
generally) viewed as a freedom from -- from suffering, from ignorance, from all the bonds which bind
us. We might sum up both viewpoints as types of
moral freedom. They differ mainly in their valua-
tions -- east, negative; west, positive -- of "this
world." The question of freedom here becomes the
question of what constitutes ethical human behavior
vis-à-vis the world, and at bottom the western and
eastern visions are not incompatible. We must free
ourselves from our limitations in order to be free
to realize our full potential.

Finally there is the peculiarly modern notion
of freedom as autonomy. Freedom here is freedom of
choice, or of action. But this idea runs into
difficulties. Consider: The more choices you face,

the more you are torn between them, i.e. the less free you are. Further, once you make the choice, you inevitably cut yourself off from other choices, other opportunities for exercising your "freedom" of choice. We might call this a freedom of the will, since it is in the exercise of human will that freedom of choice is carried out, and in mere willfulness that it is abused.

The case of Ezra Pound causes one to wonder just what happens when freedom of choice, and even freedom of movement, is denied a human being accustomed to exercising that autonomy to the full. Not many people have had the opportunity to be certified "incurably insane" by the U.S. government; how many of us would continue to write abstruse verse under such circumstances? Yet Pound picked up the pieces of his life and, after an initial period of quite understandable paranoia ("They" were in fact "coming to get him") put himself right back to work and produced some of the finest verse of his life. What does this tell us?

Ezra Pound's experience, above all his creative fortitude in the face of incredible adversity -- physical adversity at Pisa, psychological duress for 12 years at St. Elizabeth's -- mutely testifies that there must be a radical depth to human freedom which renders it possible and accessible even under the most dire constraints of nature or culture. Of course Pound is neither the first nor the last poet or writer to be unjustly imprisoned, but he does manage to project his own plight onto the Image of the human predicament in a uniquely powerful way. His "Elysium, though it were in the halls of Hell" brings to the fore the religious face of this question: Is there a freedom really free? -- unconditioned by the political, moral and egoistical considerations which seem to limit as well as define our customary notions of freedom?

Indeed. Pound's poetic odyssey -- which might otherwise seem a dead-end -- would suggest that this radical human freedom comes to light precisely when one has no choice, but... to be oneself, totally alive and awake and aware: in a word, free. Taking a cue from R. Panikkar, this unconditional freedom might best be described as the "deconditioning" of all the conditionings which condition us to accept our "unfree" condition. Is it possible in our day of factional liberations of every stripe to speak to a personal liberation of such intensity? Human Lib?(17)

If the coherence of Pound's project were just one rational "construct" or another, any stray ideological breeze might blow such a house of cards away Therefore we submit that the guiding light to that coherence in Pound's work is the unflagging creative freedom which allows him (a) to gather from the four winds the stuff of his poem, and (b) to begin anew when all is lost, Canto by Canto to cast off the past and launch himself freely into an unknown future. It is a freedom Odysseus knew, and Dante.(18) It is this freedom which testifies to the ultimate coherence, not just of one poem or another, but of Pound's life and work as a whole, his poetic odyssey as we have examined it. It is also this very freedom which allows Pound's readers to assimilate his life and work into their own. And it is this radical human freedom, finally, which may shed new light on our problematic of the "proper end" of Man:

Where do we go from here?

> Do not move
> Let the wind speak
> that is paradise.(19)

"The wind" -- read pneuma, breath, spirit -- "that is paradise" bespeaks its freedom by blowing where it will, and moving on. But hear Ezra Pound:

> Song keeps the word forever.
> Sound is moulded to mean this
> And the measure moulds sound. (20)

The human spirit thirsts for its freedom. That thirst burns in the throat, quickens, and bursts into flame. That flame is the song; at once a fragile love-song and an undying hymn of liberation. Passed heart to heart, generation to generation, and culture to culture, such singing tongues of flame constitute the tradition, the common heritage of humankind. It is a tradition of renewal:

> AS THE SUN MAKES IT NEW
> DAY BY DAY MAKE IT NEW
> YET AGAIN MAKE IT NEW (21)

EPILOGUE

Synergy of the Three Worlds

"Who even dead yet hath his mind entire!"

E.P., XLVII

A final word is in order. This poetic freedom
is all very well, it may be said, but how is it in
any way new? How is Ezra Pound's experience of
freedom unique? Did not Boethius, Villon,
Solzhenitsyn and others write eloquently from con-
finement? What does Pound add?

First of all, Ezra Pound's work stands out for
the simple reason that he does not articulate his
freedom solely in the terms of his constraint. Although much of his writing after 1945 could legitimately be construed an unjustly imprisoned man's
appeal for liberation, or at least vindication,
Pound never so much as mentions St. Elizabeth's
madhouse in The Cantos. This in itself is extraordinary. Except for descriptions of the Pisan camp
early on, and the continuing exacerbation of economic issues, his "Paradiso" emerges remarkably free
of the fairly dire straits amidst which most of it
was composed.(1) Secondly, the thrust of Pound's
novel approach is to articulate the common human
thirst for liberation in terms of the "three worlds"
which have been our concern throughout this essay.
He does not write "escapism" solely in terms of his
own plight. He attempts "to write Paradise," over
against the Image of the human predicament at large.
In this light, his work can justifiably be said to
take a more universal measure of the human predicament than, say, a call for political revolution, or
ideological revision, or prison reform, important
though these issues may be in their contexts.

One consequence of these reflections would be
to bring freedom into focus as the most basic religious category: where you find freedom, that is
religion. The most traditional path to the goal is
always unique and wholly unpredictable. In his
"Hermeneutic of Religious Freedom," R. Panikkar puts
the case somewhat as follows:

First, an act which is not free cannot be
called a religious act. A forced act would
have no religious value. The more freely an

155

act is performed, the more human and religious value it has.

Secondly, the religious act is a free act. Free in the one who performs it, and free in its effects. Religion is distinguished from its counterfeit, magic, by the fact that freedom is essential to the religious act.

...(Thus) we may reverse the classical proposition, which says that the religious act must be a free act, by emphasizing that the free act is the religious act par excellence. So it is not enough to say that an act which is not free cannot be a religious act, since the religious act is basically free; but we must add that the religiousness of the act, so to speak, comes from its freedom.(2)

In the course of this study we have been enabled by virtue of Pound's work to flesh out the primordial Image of the human predicament -- Man suspended between Earth and Heaven -- to such an extent that we now begin to discern traces of the integrity that knits the entire reality together. Pound's work introduces us to the seamless concatenation of a pluralistic reality irreducible to any of its components alone: Heaven, Man, Earth; or the theophanic, anthropological and cosmological characters of everything that arises or falls within the manifold of our experience. The ancient term synergy (literally, "working together") could perhaps stand here for the common integrity of these three worlds which constitute the entirety of our experience. As Fuller defines the term (Illustrations (b)), a synergy is a whole unpredictable from its components taken separately. The Image of the human predicament is thus transmuted from the static and alienating illusion of salvation for Man alone, to the dynamic and integrative understanding that the entire reality is always implicated in any effort toward salvation.

It tends to be forgotten that synergasia has been an important theological term for at least two millennia. St. Paul uses it (I Cor. 3:9), St. Denys refers to it(3) and, as the "semi-Pelagian heresy" of the 5th century CE, it has come to stand for the nondualistic resolution of the dispute exemplified by the entrenched Augustinian and Pelagian positions regarding redemption. There is no need to digress into dogmatics to catch the gist of the controversy. Specifically at issue is the agency involved in salvation (our question of how you get from here ("A") to there ("B") all over again). One party generally maintains that redemption comes through God's agency alone, while the other party will insist on the human ingredient. Though largely unheard of nowadays, the middle ground known as synergism is a most appealing alternative. It can be formulated as follows: "In any act of regeneration, God and Man are co-operators," i.e. synergists.

This theandric insight represents a considerable progress. And yet we today cannot but feel that something enormous has escaped consideration; namely, the whole Earth. Until just recently, western Man seems always to have pursued his goals somewhat at the expense of the Cosmos. Today we are paying for that oversight in countless ways. Pound's work, not to mention the echo of it in R.B. Fuller's discovery of "Nature's coordinate system," impels us to revise the classical synergist affirmation to include the living Cosmos:

> In any act of regeneration,
> God, Man and Cosmos are co-operators.

This re-sacralization of the secular world ought to imply a thoroughgoing recognition of the Earth as the common ground of all possible human paths to heaven: Anima Mundi.

Moreover, such a revision also reverberates on the slopes of Olympus. No longer can we justify abstracting Heaven from our human and earthly concerns. No longer can we justify fleeing "this world" for some "better place," or ignoring the plight of fellow humans in order to embrace God. No more can ends ever justify means. There is no exit from the entire reality, but there may very well be ways to enter it more deeply. What might best be called the immanent face of the divine has emerged as the most plausible resolution of the subject/object dichotomy. Less technically expressed, this means that the divine dimension presents itself as the intangible bridge over the seeming abyss that so sorely divides us from the natural world, and from one another.

Finally, Man no longer stands alone. Our fate
is bound up with the destiny of the Earth, and that
of God and the Gods as well. Our study of the poet
as psychopomp by no means leaves humankind just
betwixt and between. On the contrary, the pivotal
character of the human reality has been clarified:
"Heaven & Earth begat the perceiver." (4) Through
Pound's work we have been able to fathom somewhat
the human role as priest or mediator in the ongoing
sacred marriage of Heaven and Earth, interpreter of
the ever-recurrent hieros gamos by which all the
elements of the entire reality are colligated into a
whole. As Pound has amply demonstrated, the poet/
shaman is not just some relic of a bygone innocence,
but the architect of an integral awareness, the
hierophant who holds open the threshold to the ever-
deepening mystery of Life.

In short, our reflections on Ezra Pound's work
lead straightaway to the unabashed intuition that
the three worlds of Humankind, the Earth and the
Gods are ever embarked on a mutual adventure, each
sphere embracing the others in the freedom of their
common destiny.

That ought to be enough.

NOTES

PROLOGUE

1. Man with a capital "M" is used in the generic
sense throughout this book to denote the human
being, anthropos, homo, Mensch, Homme, and not to refer to males -- except when, as in this passage, it
also obliquely refers to Ezra Pound (as a human
being who speaks, etc.). This is done, in the first
place, for consistency with Pound's own usage and,
in the second place, because I do not believe males
have any right to a monopoly on the Name of Man
(even in English, one of the few languages where the
problem arises). In the final analysis, I suppose I
am also unwilling to concede that sexual differen-
tiation is the primary defining characteristic of
the human being.

2. Cf. Nathan SCOTT, The Broken Center, New Haven &
London (Yale Univesity Press) 1966, esp. Chapter
One, "The Name and Nature of Our Period-Style," pp.
1-24.

3. Cf. Amos N. WILDER, "The Uses of a Theological
Criticism," in Soundings: An Interdisciplinary Journal, Vol. LII, No. 1, Spring 1969, as well as T.S.
ELIOT, "Religion and Literature" and "Tradition and
the Individual Talent" in his Selected Essays, London
(Faber & Faber) 1964, for contrasting approaches to
the myriad contradictions that seem to plague the
believer as critic, and vice-versa.

4. Cf., e.g., Ernest McCLAIN, The Myth of Invariance, Boulder (Shambhala) 1978, for a rather provocative attempt to reduce several sacred literatures
to algebraic formulae.

5. Cf., e.g., the majority of essays in E.E.
ERICSON, Jr. and G.B. TENNYSON, eds., Religion and
Modern Literature: Essays in Theory and Criticism,
Grand Rapids, Michigan (Eerdmans) 1975.

6. The hermeneutic circle should be understood as a
vital circle and not a vicious one. Cf. note #14 in
Part I, Chapter 2, "The Paradise of Myth."

7. Cf. George STEINER, After Babel, Aspects of Language and Translation, London (Oxford) 1975, esp.
Chapter 1, "Understanding as Translation," pp. 1-48.

8. Cf. R. PANIKKAR, Myth, Faith and Hermeneutics, New York (Paulist Press) 1979, "Mythic Facts and Historical Facts," pp. 99-101.

9. Hans-Georg GADAMER, Truth and Method, New York (Seabury) 1976, p. 432.

10. Cf. Giles GUNN, ed., Literature and Religion, London (SCM Press) 1971. Gunn's "Introduction" and Hillis Miller's essay "The Poetry of Reality" (which forms the introduction to his own book, Poets of Reality, Cambridge (Harvard) 1965) both admirably bring into critical focus the merits as well as the weaknesses of inordinately "subjective" and "objective" studies in the field.

11. There are important exceptions. Cf., as one sign of hope, the pioneering work by Stanley Romaine HOPPER in, e.g., his "Introduction" to Interpretation: The Poetry of Meaning, New York (Harcourt, Brace & World) 1967, which also includes excellent essays by Norman O. Brown, Heinrich Ott, Owen Barfield and others. Another exemplary critic who consistently manages to break new ground without breaking utterly with tradition is of course Amos WILDER in e.g., The New Voice, New York (Herder & Herder) 1969.

12. Cf., for egregious example, Ruth Whitford's three deplorable essays on Eliot in Lee A. BELFORD, ed., Religious Dimensions in Literature, New York (Seabury) 1982. For stunning counterpoint, cf. Thomas MERTON's essay on Camus in the same volume which, instead of facile reductionism, affirms perennial religious and moral values in the works of a writer hugely skeptical of institutionalized Christianity.

13. POUND, Impact: Essays on Ignorance and the Decline of American Civilization, Noel STOCK, ed., Chicago (Henry Regnery) 1960, p. 15.

14. Cf. Mircea ELIADE, Shamanism, Princeton (Bollingen) 1972.

15. POUND, The Cantos, New York (New Directions) 1970, quoting John Heydon in Canto 91, p. 616.

NOTES

I The Walled Garden

1. Donald HALL, 'The Art of Poetry V: Ezra Pound,'
Paris Review, No. 28 (Summer/Fall 1962), 22-51, p.47.

2. William JAMES, The Varieties of Religious Experience, New York (New American Library) 1958, 'Conclusions,' p. 383: "The warring gods and formulas of
the various religions do indeed cancel each other,
but there is a certain uniform deliverance in which
religions all appear to meet. It consists of two
parts: --
   1. An uneasiness; and
   2. Its solution.
   1. The uneasiness, reduced to its simplest terms,
is a sense that there is something wrong with us as
we naturally stand.
   2. The solution is a sense that we are saved
from the wrongness by making proper connection with
the higher powers."

3. "...religion means way to salvation, ...every
religion claims to be a way to salvation." R. PANIK-
KAR, 'Hermeneutic of Religious Freedom, Religion as
Freedom,' Myth, Faith and Hermeneutics, op.cit., p.
434 et seq. This theme arises often in Panikkar's
work; he insists on the formal homology of the
various "ways to salvation." In the piece we have
cited, Panikkar continues: "Any ensemble of means
which claim to convey Man to his life's goal, however this goal might be conceived, can be considered
religion." Cf. also, R. PANIKKAR, "Have Religions
the Monopoly on Religion?," Journal of Ecumenical
Studies, Vol. XI, No. 3, Summer 1974, pp. 515-517.

4. The phrase is that of Rainier Maria RILKE, the
exposition Martin Heidegger's in 'What Are Poets
For...?' Poetry, Language, Thought, New York (Harper
& Row) 1971, A. Hofstadter trans. "If Rilke is a
'poet in a destitute time,' then only his poetry
answers the question to what end he is a poet,
whither his song is bound, where the poet belongs in
the destiny of the world's night. That destiny
decides what remains fateful within this poetry."
                                            (p.142)

5. Ingmar Bergman's haunting film of the same name
is the most recent appearance of a phrase which is
also pivotal in Dickens (Our Mutual Friend) and

Melville (Pierre, or the Ambiguities). The reference is to the hour just preceding the dawn.

6. From muein, the myth is mute; the unspoken. Cf.
R. PANIKKAR, 'Faith, A Constitutive Human Dimension,' Myth, Faith and Hermeneutics, op.cit.: "And
myth is myth because it is muein and not legein,
mute and not speaking." (p. 188)

7. Cf. Gregory BATESON, Steps Toward An Ecology of
Mind, New York (Dutton) 1975, and Mind & Nature: A
Necessary Unity New York (Dutton) 1979. From the
Introduction to the latter, published in Co-Evolu-
tion Quarterly No. 18 (Summer 1978), p. 11; "I offer
you the notion of context, i.e. pattern through
time." "...without context there is no meaning."

8. Cf. R. PANIKKAR, 'Śunaḥśepa, A Myth of the Human
Condition,' Myth, Faith and Hermeneutics, op.cit.,
p. 98 et seq.

9. The phrase "myths of paradise" is used here in
the privative sense, to refer to the traditional
paradises "lost" by modern Man.

10. Recall that Faust was originally a marionette in
a puppet-show, and the paradoxical position of "ab-
surd Man" or modern Man is established in a single
image. To some extent, the drama of this theme in
the original Faust is weakened in Goethe's version
where, after all, Faust is caught up into heaven
amid multiple hosannahs.

11. Ezra POUND, 'Drafts & Fragments,' The Cantos,
op.cit., p. 802.

12. Norman O. BROWN, Love's Body, New York (Vintage) 1966, p. 262. The entire chapter XVI, 'Nothing' is à propos.

13. Cf. J.P. SARTRE's play No Exit (Huit Clos,
Paris, 1944) and A. CAMUS' essay The Myth of
Sisyphus, New York (Vintage) 1965.

14. Cf. M. HEIDEGGER, Sein und Zeit, Erste Hälfte,
in Jahrbuch fur Philosophie und Phänomenologische
Forschung (Halle) 1926, VIII, 1-438. The hermeneutical circle, or circuit, is in no sense a "vicious"
one, e.g., p. 315: "The effort should much rather

be to leap into the 'circle' in an original and thoroughgoing way..." (Wm. J. Richardson, trans.)

15. Cf. S.R. HOPPER, 'Jerusalem's Walls and Other Perimeters,' Humanities, Religion and the Arts Tomorrow, H. Hunter, ed., New York (Holt, Rinehard & Winston) 1972.

16. Cf. F.W.J. SCHELLING, System of Transcendental Idealism, some relevant portions of which have been translated in FELDMAN & RICHARDSON, The Rise of Modern Mythology, Bloomington (Indiana University Press) 1972, e.g., p. 322: "...how a new mythology (which cannot be the invention of an individual poet but only of a new generation that represents things as if it were a single poet) can itself arise, is a problem for whose solution we must look to the future destiny of the world." (1800)

17. Demythicization always implies remythicization, as R. PANIKKAR puts it in "The Myth of Morals and the Moral of Myth," Myth, Faith and Hermeneutics, op.cit., pp. 37-64.

18. POUND, Canto LXXIV, p. 425.

19. M. HEIDEGGER, 'The Way to Language,' On the Way to Language, New York (Harper & Row) 1971. The phrase is recurrent with Heidegger; this entire essay is relevant. Cf. also 'The Principle of Identity,' Identity and Difference, New York (Harper & Row) 1969, e.g., pp. 32-33.

20. T.S. ELIOT, 'Little Gidding,' Four Quartets, New York (Harcourt, Brace & World) 1943/1971, p. 59:

> "We shall not cease from exploration
> And the end of all our exploring
> Will be to arrive where we started
> And know the place for the first time."

21. The literature on the return is enormous, running in the West from Gilgamesh to its perigee during the past hundred years in NIETZSCHE's "eternal return of the Same," Cf. Thus Spoke Zarathustra, Second Part, 'The Stillest Hour,' in The Portable Nietzsche, New York (Viking) 1968, Walter KAUFMAN trans. Cf. also M. HEIDEGGER's treatment of F. Hölderlin's poem Homecoming in 'Remembrance of the Poet,' Existence and Being, Chicago (Gateway) 1949, Werner Brock trans.

22. "...myth offers the subsoil from which differing philosophical systems may draw sustenance." R. PANIKKAR, 'Śunaḥśepa, A Myth of the Human Condition,' Myth, Faith and Hermeneutics, op.cit., p. 98.

23. Cf. Part II, Chapter 8.

24. Gilgamesh antedates Homer, to be sure, but the various tablet-texts of Gilgamesh were unearthed in 19th century archeological excavations and can be said to have had only a dilute influence on classical Mediterranean literature. Cf. N.K. SANDERS, The Epic of Gilgamesh, Baltimore (Penguin) 1960, Introduction, 'Discovery of the Tablets,' pp. 9-12.

25. Cf. Erwin ROHDE, Psyche, The Cult of Souls and Belief in Immortality among the Greeks, Vols. I&II, New York (Harper & Row) 1966, W.K.C. Guthrie, trans. Part I, Chapter I deals with the Homeric material.

26. POUND, Canto 93, p. 632.

27. James JOYCE, Ulysses, New York (Vintage/Random House) 1961.

28. Nikos KAZANTZAKIS, The Odyssey, A Modern Sequel, New York (Simon & Schuster) 1958, Kimon Friar trans.

29. POUND, Canto 91, p. 617.

30. "The Homeric picture of the shadow-life of the disembodied soul (psyche) is the work of resignation, not of hope... one which promised only a restless, purposeless fluttering to and fro, an existence, indeed, but without any of the content that might have made it worthy of the name of life." E. ROHDE, Psyche, op.cit., Vol. I, Chapter II, p. 55.

31. POUND, e.g., the last line of the 'Thrones,' Canto 109, p. 774.

32. Cf. SOPHOCLES, Oedipus Trilogy; any translation of the trilogy is sufficient to give the sense of Tiresias' pivotal role.

33. POUND, the first line of Canto XLVII, p. 236.

34. In his rendering of this episode (Canto I) Pound had either the good sense or the sheer nerve

(depending on one's critical perspective) to edit
out most of Tiresias' oration, including these lines
(120-134) obliquely prophetic of his own fate in his
own land:

> "Then you must take up your well-shaped oar and
> go on a journey/ until you come to where there
> are men living who know nothing/ of the sea,
> and who eat food that is not mixed with salt,
> who never/ have known well-shaped oars, which
> act for ships as wings do./
>
> "And I will tell you a very clear proof, and
> you cannot miss it./ When, as you walk, some
> other wayfarer happens to meet you,/ and says
> you carry a winnow-fan on your bright shoulder,
> /then you must plant your well-shaped oar in
> the ground, and render/ ceremonious sacrifice
> to the lord Poseidon,/ ...and make your way
> home again and render holy hecatombs/ to the
> immortal gods who hold open the wide heaven,
> /all of them in order."

From Richmond LATTIMORE, The Odyssey of Homer, A
Modern Translation, New York (Harper & Row) 1965, p.
171.

35. POUND, Canto XLVII, p. 236.

36. "Rupture of planes" is one of the ways Mircea
Eliade has often chosen to characterize initiation.
Cf. The Sacred and the Profane, New York (Harcourt,
Brace & World) 1959.

37. Cf. R. PANIKKAR, 'Sunahśepa,' Part 3.2.1.3,
Myth, Faith and Hermeneutics, op.cit., p. 161.

38. The reference is to Glaukos, whom, as Dante
notes ('Paradiso,' Canto I, 68-69), after tasting of
a certain herb, "to the other sea-gods... was made
akin." L. Binyon trans., Portable Dante, New York
(Viking) 1952, p. 369.

39. The Homeric sense of this "craft" is double:
There is Odysseus' raft, the vessel or medium by
which he is conveyed from here to there. And Odysseus himself is described as "craft, wily," a translation for polymetis: a polymath. A third sense is
added by Pound's own insistence on technique -- tekné,
craft -- in the discipline of writing poetry.

40. Cf. R. LATTIMORE, The Odyssey of Homer, op.cit.,
Bk. X.

41. Companions of Odysseus.

42. The blind seer of the Oedipus trilogy, who
prophesied that Oedipus would slay his father and
marry his mother.

43. This place.

44. The God of this place.

45. His consort.

46. Elpenor, who fell to his death from Circe's
ingle. I have omitted this section of Canto I, as
well as some of the beginning and some of the conclusion of Pound's rendering. (Cf. also Part II,
Chapter 7b.)
Elpenor dictates his own epitaph, "A man of no
fortune, and with a name to come," which Pound
applies to himself in the Pisan Cantos.

47. Anticlea, Odysseus' mother, with whom he speaks
after hearing Tiresias.

48. Excerpted and abridged from POUND, The Cantos,
op.cit., Canto I, pp. 3-5. The speaker is Odysseus,
rendered by Pound in the alliterative Anglo-Saxon
rhythms of The Seafarer. Cf. POUND, 'The Seafarer'
(1912), Translations, New York (New Directions)
1963, pp. 207-9.
One of the most thoroughgoing explications of this
passage is Hugh KENNER's in The Pound Era, Berkeley
(University of California Press) 1971, 'The Cantos -
I', p. 349 et. seq. Kenner's work on Pound is impec-
cable and quite invaluable; we shall be referring to
it often.

II The Word As Image*

*The tripartite schema of Part II owes the great part of its inspiration to R. PANIKKAR, Colligite Fragmenta, Toward An Integration of Reality, New York (Villanova Univ.) 1978, e.g., p. 74: "The cosmotheandric principle could be stated by saying that the divine, the human and the earthly -- however we may prefer to call them -- are the three irreducible dimensions which constitute the real, i.e. any reality inasmuch as it is real."

A/ Cosmological Patterns

1. POUND, 'Affirmations, IV' The New Age, 28 Jan. 1915, p. 349.

2. KENNER, Pound Era, op.cit., pp. 157-8. Cf. also R.W. EMERSON's essays 'The Method of Nature' (1841) and 'The Poet' (1844).

3. POUND, 'Don'ts for Imagistes,' Poetry, 1913, reprinted in POUND, Literary Essays, New York (New Directions) 1968, p. 5. Cf. also W.C. Williams' famous dictum: "No ideas/ but in things." A more recent excursus on the same theme can be found in the chapter "The New Science of Language" in Norman O. Brown's Closing Time, New York (Vintage) 1973, p. 99:
"It is all one book
The Book of God's Works and the Book of God's Word.
Every phenomenon is scripture
not alphabetic but hieroglyphic."

4. POUND, 'The Tree,' Personae, The Collected Shorter Poems of Ezra Pound (1926), New York (New Directions) 1971, p.3.

5. The tale of Baucis and Philemon turning into intertwining trees, for example, is told in Ovid's Metamorphoses. They surface again at the beginning of Canto 90.

6. Cf. KENNER, 'Knot & Vortex,' Pound Era, op.cit., p.145 et seq., and throughout his study, e.g., from p.290: "Metamorphosis -- identity persisting through change -- gives the rationale of 'artistic unity'; in music, the key; in painting, the harmony within which 'the farthest and faintest influence of each potent tint melts into the enormous sum of the influences of all,' and 'every color modifies every other'; in poetry, the control of metaphorical over-tones, the 'halos of secondary meaning' which vi-brate 'with physical wealth and the warm wealth of man's nature,' and yet must 'blend into a fabric as pure as crystal'." (Quotations from Ernest FENOLLOSA, The Chinese Written Character As a Medium for Poetry, San Francisco (City Lights) 1936/1968, which we discuss below.)

7. Cf. Paul RICOEUR, 'Parole et Symbole,' in Le Symbole, Strasbourg (Faculté de Theologie Catholique, Palais Universitaire) 1975, pp.142-61, particularly his discussion of the "tensile" character of metaphor and symbol. Cf. also RICOEUR, The Rule of the Metaphor, 'Multidisciplinary Studies of the Creation of Meaning in Language,' Toronto (Univ. of Toronto) 1978, Czerny trans.

8. Ernest FENOLLOSA, The Chinese Written Character as a Medium for Poetry, op. cit.

9. Ibid., pp.22-3. Cf. also Norman O. BROWN, Love's Body, op.cit., p.266: "Everything is only a meta-phor; there is only poetry."

10. Ibid., pp.23-4. Fenollosa/Pound continues: "Our ancestors built the accumulations of metaphor into structures of language and into systems of thought. Languages today are thin and cold because we think less and less into them. We are forced, for the sake of quickness and sharpness, to file each word to its narrowest edge of meaning. Nature would seem

to have become less and less like a paradise and
more and more like a factory...
"Only scholars and poets feel painfully back along
the thread of our etymologies and piece together our
diction, as best they may, from forgotten fragments.
This anaemia of modern speech is only too well
encouraged by the feeble force of our phonetic symbols. There is little or nothing in a phonetic word
to exhibit the embryonic stages of its growth. It
does not bear its metaphor on its face. We forget
that personality once meant not the soul, but the
soul's mask. This is the sort of thing one can not
possibly forget in using the Chinese symbols."

11. An interesting direction of inquiry into Pound's
work based on the principle of metonymy has been
developed, employing criteria derived often from
Jacques Derrida, Roland Barthes and of course Claude
Levi-Strauss, but this is not our topic. How does
the notion of metonymy apply to Pound? When I say
"Knife," and you take it into your head to respond
"Fork," you have made a metonymic association. Members of a group or series evoke the "set" of which
they are elements, as do certain lines, words and
phrases in Pound.

12. POUND, Guide to Kulchur, New York (New Directions)
1970, Chapter 2, 'The New Learning, Part One,' p.23 et
seq.

13. Cf. POUND, 'I Gather the Limbs of Osiris,' in
Ezra Pound, Selected Prose, New York (New Directions) 1973 (reprinted from The New Age, 7 Dec.
1911), 'A Rather Dull Introduction,' pp.21-4: "When
I speak of a 'New Method in Scholarship', I do not
imagine that I am speaking of a method by me discovered. I mean, merely, a method not of common
practice, a method not yet clearly or consciously
formulated, a method which has been intermittently
used by all good scholars since the beginning of
scholarship, the method of Luminous Detail, a method
most vigorously hostile to the prevailing mode today
-- that is, the method of multitudinous detail, and
to the method of yesterday, the method of sentiment
and generalization. The latter is too inexact and
the former too cumbersome to be of much use to the
normal man wishing to live mentally active."...
"Any fact is, in a sense, 'significant'. Any fact
may be 'symptomatic', but certain facts give one a
sudden insight into circumjacent conditions, into
their causes, their effects, into sequence, and law."...

"In the history of the development of civilisation
or literature, we come upon such interpreting detail. A few dozen facts of this nature give us
intelligence of a period -- a kind of intelligence
not to be gathered from a great array of facts of
the other sort. These facts are hard to find. They
are swift and easy of transmission. They govern
knowledge as the switchboard governs an electric
current."

14. Le mot juste -- the "proper" word -- is an
untranslatable phrase supposed to have originated
with Flaubert. Pound used it often. However, one
of Hugh Kenner's diligent graduate students recently
undertook to read all of Flaubert (including letters, etc.) in search of "le mot juste," and did not
locate the phrase.

15. FENOLLOSA, Chinese Written Character, op.cit.,
p.12. Cf. also the discussion of la virtù in POUND,
'Introduction' to Cavalcanti, Translations, New York
(New Directions) 1963, pp.17-20.

16. Cf. Part II, Chapters 4-6.

17. POUND, Canto I, p.4.

18. FENOLLOSA, Chinese Written Character, op.cit.,
p.29.

19. POUND, ABC of Reading, New York (New Directions)
1936/1960, Chapter One, in which he dissociates from
Fenollosa's observations a method, for reading and
writing.

20. FENOLLOSA, op.cit., p.13.

21. POUND, 'Affirmations, IV,' The New Age, op.cit.,
loc.cit.

22. FENOLLOSA, op.cit., p. 31.

23. Cf. KENNER, Pound Era, op.cit., pp.290-1:
"...for the best Chinese poems Fenollosa claims
simply that to their technique of sound (which his
notes discuss at length) they add both visual grace
and visual reinforcement of the metaphors everywhere
flashing. 'The elements of the overtones vibrate
against the eye,' and 'the frequent return of the
same element into new combinations makes possible a
choice of words in which the same tone interpene-

trates and colors every plane of meaning.'"
(Cf. also the discussion of frequency in our Chapter
8b).

24. S.R. HOPPER, 'Le Cri de Merlinl,' Anagogic
Qualities of Literature, Joseph STRELKA, ed., Year-
book of Comparative Literature, Vol. IV, University
Park, Pennsylvania (Penn. State University) 1971, p.25.

25. POUND, The Spirit of Romance, New York (New
Directions) 1968, p.87.

26. Ibid., pp.92-3.

27. POUND, 'Medievalism,' Literary Essays, New York
(New Directions), 1968, p.154.

28. Cf. POUND, A Memoir of Gaudier-Brzeska, New York
(New Directions) 1970.

29. POUND, Canto 95, p.645.

30. POUND, 'Medievalism," Literary Essays, op.cit.,
loc.cit. Cf. also Walter BAUMANN, The Rose in the
Steel Dust, An Examination of the Cantos of Ezra
Pound, Bern (Francke Verlag) 1967, an altogether
admirable study of the "pattern" that comes to light
in (mainly two of) Pound's Cantos.

31. A Lume Spento (With Tapers Quenched), POUND's
first book of poems, published at his own expense in
Venice, June 1908.

32. In 'Sestina: Altaforte,' Personae, op.cit., p.28.

33. In Canto II.

34. In Canto 93.

35. In, e.g., Canto XIII. See also our Chapters 4-6
for the Confucian background.

36. E.g., Canto I.

37. The phrasing is mine, the intuition that of
R. PANIKKAR, in Colligite Fragmenta, op.cit., and
elsewhere.

38. POUND, Confucius, New York (New Directions)
1968, p.36.

39. Cf. M. HEIDEGGER, Being and Time, op.cit., On
the Way to Language, op.cit., and perhaps above all,
'The Origin of the Work of Art,' in Poetry, Language, Thought, New York (Harper & Row) 1971, where
he discusses the work of art as "the fitting or
joining of the shining of truth." Cf. also S.R.
HOPPER, 'Le Cri de Merlin!,' op.cit. Also of interest are several of the essays contained in J.J.
KOCKELMANS, ed., On Heidegger and Language, Evanston, Illinois (Northwestern Univ. Press) 1972, e.g.,
W. BIEMEL, 'Poetry and Language in Heidegger,' O.
PÖGGELER, 'Heidegger's Topology of Being,' and H.
BIRAULT, 'Thinking and Poetizing in Heidegger.'

40. Incident related in Marie de RACHEWILTZ, Discretions, Boston (Atlantic/Little Brown) 1971.

41. Cf. S.R. HOPPER, 'Jerusalem's Walls and Other
Perimeters,' op.cit.

42. For a discussion of "lux in diafana," cf.
'Medievalism,' POUND, Literary Essays, op.cit.

43. A term especially popular as it applies to J.
JOYCE's early technique in Dubliners, and A Portrait
of the Artist As a Young Man.

44. E.g., by Noel STOCK in the final chapters of The
Life of Ezra Pound, New York (Pantheon/Random House)
1970.

2 Image

1. First published in the collection Lustra, this
tiny but much-discussed poem can be found on p. 109
of POUND, Personae, op.cit.

2. Lewis UNTERMEYER, ed., Modern American and Modern
British Poetry, New York (Harcourt, Brace & World)
1955, p.157.

3. Cf. 'A Retrospect,' Literary Essays, op.cit.,
pp.3-14, which collects some of POUND's early Imagiste writings (e.g. 'A Few Don'ts for Imagistes')
and provides a good survey of the state of the art
circa 1918. Cf. also H.N. SCHNEIDAU, Ezra Pound:
The Image and the Real, Baton Rouge (Louisiana State
Univ. Press) 1969, for this period.

4. KENNER, Pound Era, op.cit., pp.184-5.

5. Cf. Earl MINER, 'Pound, Haiku, and the Image,'
Hudson Review, IX (Winter, 1956-57), pp.570-84.

6. The first line of 'A Few Don'ts,' From Poetry,
I,6 (March, 1913), reprinted in 'A Retrospect,'
Literary Essays, op.cit., p.4.

7. As I did, late in the summer of 1969, with this
poem in mind. I had not at the time read Pound's
prose account cited above. I had only the little
poem to guide me. Years later, it strikes me that
what I happened to see in the underground was probably as much the product of my own imagination as of
Pound's; else I suspect he would have related the
event somewhat differently in T.P.'s Weekly. Yet I
have also come to believe that Pound wrote the poem
the way that he did precisely in order to stimulate
some such reciprocal adventure of the spirit, so I
shall relate the story just as it befell me, with a
few critical interpolations. As Pound put it: "An
image... is real because we know it directly."
Gaudier-Brzeska, op.cit., p.86.

8. KENNER, Pound Era, op.cit., loc.cit.

9. Cf. William Carlos WILLIAMS, Kora in Hell, New
York (New Directions) 1965.

10. KENNER, Pound Era, op.cit., loc.cit.

11. I.e., an inheritance from the French symboliste movement of the late 19th century. Cf., e.g., Arthur RIMBAUD, 'Une Saison En Enfer,' in Oeuvres Poétique d'Arthur Rimbaud, Paris (Garnier-Flammarion) 1964. The Louise Varèse translation is serviceable and available with a good selection of other symboliste works in J.M. BERNSTEIN, ed., Baudelaire, Rimbaud, Verlaine, New York (Citadel) 1965.

12. POUND, Gaudier-Brzeska, op.cit., p. 89.

13. Donald DAVIE, Ezra Pound, Poet As Sculptor, New York (Oxford) 1964, pp.56-7.

14. There are Daniel translations in POUND, Translations, op.cit., The Spirit of Romance (II,III,&V), op.cit., and under 'Arnaut Daniel' in Literary Essays, op.cit., pp.109-48.

15. POUND, The Spirit of Romance, op.cit., e.g., p.97.

16. KENNER, Pound Era, op.cit., p.184.

17. Cf. Claude LEVI-STRAUSS, The Raw and the Cooked, New York (Harper & Row) 1970, J.&D. Weightman, trans., for the most celebrated application of "structuralist" techniques to mythic material.

18. Cf. Roland BARTHES, Elements of Semiology, London (Cape) 1967.

19. POUND, Canto 106, p.752.

20. POUND, Canto XLVII, P.238.

21. Letter to Homer L. Pound, 11 April 1927, in The Letters of Ezra Pound, D.D. PAIGE, ed., New York (Harcourt, Brace & World) 1950.

22. As it is for D. PEARLMAN, in The Barb of Time, On the Unity of Ezra Pound's Cantos, New York/London (Oxford) 1969, for example.

23. The original reads "seemed" rank folly; revised versions read "was" rank folly.

24. One of Pound's own epithets for St. Elizabeth's Hospital in Washington, D.C., where he survived 12 years captivity.

25. Levi-Strauss's term for a myth-maker -- brico-leur, "fix-it-man" -- cf. LEVI-STRAUSS, The Savage Mind, Chicago (Univ. of Chicago) 1970, Chapter 1.

26. POUND, Canto 93, p.631.

27. Cf. POUND, 'The Phantom Dawn,' Spirit of Romance, op.cit., Chapter 1.

28. This view of imagination as picture thinking is still current in British analytical linguistic philosophy. Cf. the words of B. Russell, G. Ryle, L. Ayer, et al.

29. Cf. M. HEIDEGGER, On the Way to Language, op.cit., p.123.

30. Cf. KENNER, Pound Era, op.cit., especially the chapters 'Knot & Vortex,' 'Transformations.'

31. Cheng ming, the Confucian doctrine of the "rec-tification of terminology," which we shall discuss at length in Chapter 6.

32. Cf. Jose ARGÜELLES, The Transformative Vision, Berkeley (Shambhala) 1972. From Chapter 2: "The 'error' of the Renaissance perceptual model was in forgetting the whole, or the Unity, thus causing the plunge of consciousness into particles -- the parti-cularization of matter into atoms of knowledge and informational bits, and humanity into individuals." ... "If art is no longer specialized, then art becomes a means of relating to the whole."

33. Cf. M. HEIDEGGER, 'Origin of the Work of Art,' Poetry, Language, Thought, op.cit., pp.15-88.

34. POUND, Gaudier-Brzeska op.cit., p.86. The full quotation is carried in our Illustrations.

3 Vortex

1. POUND, Gaudier-Brzeska, op.cit., p.92.

2. "Henri Gaudier-Brzeska: after months of fighting and two promotions for gallantry, Henri Gaudier-Brzeska was killed in a charge at Neuville St. Vaaste, on June 5th, 1915,", cited in POUND, Gaudier-Brzeska, op.cit., p.17.

3. Cf. KENNER, Pound Era., op.cit., p.240: "And the arch-Vorticist was Lewis unmistakably. Without him, the movement is inconceivable..."

4. Our focus here is on the image VORTEX itself rather more than on the ups and downs of the movement comprised of Pound, Epstein, Gaudier, Lewis and others. Kenner's treatment of Vorticism in The Pound Era remains the most inclusive and deserves the reader's full attention. 'Vortex Lewis,' p.232 et seq. is especially worthwhile. Cf. also Gaudier-Brzeska, Drawings and Sculpture, New York (October House) 1965. It is also noteworthy that the ending sequence of Ken Russell's film on Gaudier -- The Savage Messiah, a colorful but historically useless production for BBC -- is an astonishing tour of a room filled with what amounts to Gaudier's life's work, or at least as complete a collection as has ever been assembled.

5. KENNER, Pound Era, op.cit., p.239.

6. "Vector Equilibrium" is R.B. FULLER's name for the Archimedean cuboctahedron. Vector equilibria in Fuller's synergetic geometry are not, however, "solids," but rather centers, event foci. It can be said that the vector equilibrium is the zero of the synergetic geometry. See our Illustrations. The most thoroughgoing exposition is Fuller's own in Chapter 4, 'System,' of Synergetics, Explorations in the Geometry of Thinking, R.B. FULLER & E.J. APPLEWHITE, New York (Macmillan) 1975.

7. Wyndham Lewis apparently coined the rock-drill phrase, and Pound picked it up to title the first installment of post-Pisan Cantos 'Section Rock-Drill, 85-95, de los Cantares.'

8. Pound often referred to Gaudier as "the clearest case of genius I ever met" -- which, for Pound, is saying something.

9. POUND's review of UPWARD's Divine Mystery appeared in The New Freewoman (The Egoist), 15 Nov. 1913. His article 'Allen Upward Serious,' concerning Upward's The New Word, appeared in The New Age, 23 April 1914.

10. Donald DAVID, Ezra Pound, New York (Viking) 1975, pp.66-8.

11. Ibid., p.67.

12. Ibid.

13. Pound met Fuller in Venice, October 1970, while Fuller was lecturing at the Venice International University of Art. KENNER notes that "part of Fuller's subject was Ezra Pound.", Pound Era, op.cit., pp.559-60.

14. Cf. R.B. FULLER & E.J. APPLEWHITE, Synergetics, op.cit, paragraphs 931.6 to 934.03, pp.519-24. And also FULLER, No More Secondhand God, New York (Doubleday) 1971, the final chapter, 'Omnidirectional Halo,' pp.105-45.

15. DAVIE, Ezra Pound, op.cit., pp.66-7. Cf. also W.B. YEATS, A Vision, New York (Macmillan) 1937, where the gyres are reminiscent of this vortex. There is also reference to a "double vortex" of interlocking cones in Book II, 'The Completed Symbol,' Chapter XIV, p.209.

16. FENOLLOSA, The Chinese Written Character, op.cit., p.12.

17. Allen UPWARD, The Divine Mystery, Letchworth (Garden City Press) 1913, recently re-released by Capra Press.

18. Cf. E.A.S. BUTTERWORTH, The Tree at the Navel of the Earth, Berlin (Walter De Gruyter & Co.) 1970. Cf. also the chapter 'Internal Technology' in J. ARGÜELLES' Transformative Vision, op.cit. M. ELIADE's Shamanism, op.cit., remains the classic study.

19. Cf. Eva HESSE, 'Frobenius As Rainmaker,' Paideuma, Vol.I, No.1, pp. 85-8.

20. UPWARD, Divine Mystery, op.cit., p.1.

21. Cf. also the cosmotheandric intuition of R. PANIKKAR, Colligite Fragmenta, op.cit.

22. POUND, Canto 99, p.698.

23. UPWARD, Divine Mystery, op.cit., pp.308-9.

24. Cf. POUND, Personae, op.cit., p.187, from the Mauberley sequence:

"E.P. Ode Pour L'election de Son Sepulchre

For three years, out of key with his time,
He strove to resuscitate the dead art
Of poetry; to maintain 'the sublime'
In the old sense. Wrong from the start--

No, hardly, but seeing he had been born
In a half savage country, out of date;
Bent resolutely on wringing lilies from the acorn..."

*EXHIBIT: VORTEX, By Henri Gaudier-Brzeska, from POUND, Gaudier-Brzeska, op.cit., pp.20-24.

B/ Anthropological Paradigms

4 Pivot

1. POUND, Confucius, New York (New Directions) 1951,
pp.173-5.

2. Or rather, "Elder Lightfoot is not downhearted
            Elder Lightfoot is cert'nly
                        not
                           downhearted.
        He observes a design in the Process."
POUND, Canto 95, p.645.

3. Cf. POUND, Gaudier-Brzeska, op.cit., pp.75-127.

4. Cf. Sidney GEIST, Brancusi, The Sculpture and Drawings, New York (Harry N. Abrams, Inc.) 1975, for a
survey of Brancusi' work.

5. POUND, 'Brancusi' (1921), Literary Essays, op.cit.,
pp.441-6.

6. Cf. Donald DAVIE, Ezra Pound, Poet As Sculptor,
op.cit.

7. The Greek perichoresis -- along with the latin
circumincessio -- are terms used in the scholastic
tradition to describe the relationship pertaining
among the three "persons" or "characters" of the Trinity.

8. Cf. Norman O. BROWN, Hermes the Thief, New York
(Vintage) 1970.

9. POUND, 'Brancusi,' Literary Essays, op.cit., p.442.
POUND also writes (in his Gaudier-Brzeska, op.cit.,
pp.155-6) of Lewis, Epstein, Gaudier et al.: "These
new men have made me see form, have made me more
conscious of the appearance of the sky where it juts
down between houses, of the bright pattern of sunlight
which the bath water throws up on the ceiling, of the
great "V's" of light that dart through the chinks over
the curtain rings, all these are new chords, new keys
of design."

10. Cf. Mircea ELIADE on "ec-stasis" and the three
worlds in Shamanism, op.cit., especially Chapter
VIII, 'Shamanism and Cosmology,' pp.259-87. Cf.
also M. ELIADE, Yoga -- Immortality and Freedom,

New York (Bollingen) 1958, for the "en-static" inter-
iorization of this process.

11. Cf., mainly for purposes of comparison, Y.L. FUNG,
A History of Chinese Philosophy, D. Bodde trans.,
Vol.I, New York (Princeton) 1952; or W.-T. CHAN, A
Sourcebook in Chinese Philosophy, New York (Princeton)
1963.

12. More familiar at least to readers of English.

13. Cf. Martin HEIDEGGER's use of the term "Ereignis"
as "event of appropriation," in Poetry, Language,
Thought, op.cit., and On the Way to Language, op.cit.
Cf. also W.J. RICHARDSON, Heidegger -- Through Phenomenology to Thought, the Hague (Martinus Nijhoff)
1963, pp.401-620.

14. The Four Books are: The Great Learning (Ta Hsio),
The Unwobbling Pivot (Chung Yung), The Analects, and
the Book of Mencius. The selection from the vast
array of stone texts was made by the famous 12th
century Neo-Confucian scholar Chu Hsi.

15. POUND (trans.), Confucius, op.cit., 'Tsze Tsze's
First Thesis,' p.103.

16. Cf. J. CORNELL, The Trial of Ezra Pound: A Documented Account of the Treason Case By the Defendant's
Lawyer, New York (John Day Co.) 1966.

17. Metanoia, the familiar "Repent!" of the street
preacher, originally denoted a complete change of
nous -- mind, heart and soul.

18. The great exception is of course Richard WILHELM,
whose insight into the Confucian tradition as a whole
is matched only by his extraordinarily acute translation of the I Ching, Cary F. Baynes, trans., New York
(Princeton) 1969. Cf. also his Confucius & Confucianism, New York (Harcourt, Brace & World) 1931, and
WILHELM/JUNG, The Secret of the Golden Flower, New
York (Harcourt, Brace & World) 1962.

19. But he did not produce verses merely bemoaning his
fate; he tightened up his Confucian translations.
"Historical tragedy, for Pound, is the result of so-
ciety's loss of harmony with the process.", PEARLMAN,
Barb of Time, op.cit., p.244. Cf. also N. STOCK, The
Life of Ezra Pound, op.cit., Chapters XVIII - XXI.

20. KENNER, Pound Era, op.cit., p.448.

21. POUND wrote a rather tedious opera from Villon's Testament before the war; the original written just before the author's execution.

22. POUND (trans.), from 'The Great Learning' (Ta Hsio), Confucius, op.cit., pp.27-8.

5 Rite

1. Herbert FINGARETTE, Confucius--the Secular As Sacred, New York (Harper & Row) 1972, Chapter 1, p.7: "The novel and creative insight of Confucius was to see this aspect of human existence, its form as learned tradition and convention, in terms of a particular revelatory image: li, i.e. 'holy rite,' 'sacred ceremony,' in the usual meaning of the term prior to Confucius."

2. Cf. Arthur WALEY, The Analects of Confucius, New York (Random House) 1938.

3. Hugh KENNER, in his 'Introduction' to POUND's Translations, op.cit., p.14: "Behind certain ideograms in the Confucian Analects Mr. Arthur Waley sensed a sage embroidered on tapestry expounding the Way:

'The Master said, Who expects to be able to go out of a house except by the door? How is it then that no one follows this Way of ours?'
And Pound a live man speaking pregnant sense:
'He said: The way out is via the door, how is it that no one will use this method?'"

4. Cf. also FINGARETTE, Confucius, op.cit., pp.7-10, and pp.16-17, where he sums up as follows: "The image of Holy Rite (li) as a metaphor of human existence brings foremost to our attention the dimension of the holy in man's existence. ... Confucius wanted to teach, as a corollary, that sacred ceremony in its narrower, root meaning is not a totally mysterious appeasement of spirits external to human and earthly life. Spirit is no longer an external being influenced by the ceremony; it is that that is expressed and comes most alive in the ceremony. Instead of being diversion of attention from the human realm to another transcendent realm, the overtly holy ceremony is to be seen as the central symbol, both expressive of and participating in the holy as a dimension of all truly human existence."

5. Ibid., p.17.

6. J. NEEDHAM, Science and Civilization in China, Cambridge (Cambridge University Press) 1956, cited by Fritjof CAPRA, The Tao of Physics, Boulder (Shambhala) 1976, p.280.

7. FINGARETTE, Confucius, op.cit., p. 19.

8. POUND, Confucius, op.cit., p.147.

9. FINGARETTE, Confucius, op.cit., p.55.

10. Drawing from ibid., Chapters 2 and 3, 'A Way Without A Crossroads' and 'The Locus of the Personal.'

11. POUND, Confucius, op.cit., 'Ta Hsio I,' p.27.

12. Ibid., 'Chung Yung,' p.179.

13. Ibid., 'Ta Hsio,' pp.29-33.

14. Ibid., p.22. The gloss continues: "...the man and his full contents."

15. Cf. José ORTEGA Y GASSET, What is Philosophy?, New York (Norton) 1960, especially the final three chapters.

16. FINGARETTE, Confucius, op.cit., pp.46-7.

17. Ibid., p.42.

18. Ibid., p.56.

19. POUND, Translations, op.cit., p.18. This should perhaps be emended; in our day of rampant nuclear proliferation, we know all too well that what radium displays is a quite ignoble virtù of energy, but virtù nonetheless.

20. Cf. Thomas MERTON, Mystics & Zen Masters, New York (Harper & Row) 1972, whose understanding of the Confucian tradition, he avows, owes much to Ezra Pound.

21. POUND, Confucius, op.cit., p.109.

*EXHIBIT excerpted from 'The Temple Odes of Chou,' 1. Ts'ing Miao, in E. POUND, trans., The Confucian Odes, New York (New Directions) 1954, pp.198-9.

1. POUND, Confucius, op.cit., 'Chung Yung,' p.127.

2. POUND, Guide to Kulchur, New York (New Directions) 1970.

3. POUND, from 'A Retrospect' (Pavannes & Divagations, Literary Essays, op.cit., p.9. Cf. also Christine BROOKE-ROSE, A ZBC Of Ezra Pound, Berkeley (UC Press) 1971. Ms. Brooke-Rose recognizes that Pound's attitude toward technique presupposes the necessary unity of "form" and "content," those twin bugaboos of an obsolete aestheticism. She cites Susan Sontag's essay on Style:
> "It would be hard to find any reputable literary critic who would care to be caught defending as an idea the antithesis of style versus content. Everyone is quick to avow that style and content are indissoluble, that the strongly individual style of each important writer is an organic aspect of his work and never something merely 'decorative.'
> "In the practice of criticism, though, the old antithesis lives on, virtually unassailed."*
*From S. SONTAG, Against Interpretation, London 1967.

4. Cf. KENNER, Pound Era, op.cit., p.452:
(Pound) "誠 'Sincerity.' The precise definition of the word, pictorially the sun's lance coming to rest on the precise spot verbally. The right-hand half of this compound means: to perfect, bring to focus." (Confucius, op.cit., p.20).

(Kenner) "That the lance should be the sun's, that 'perfect' should mean 'bring to focus,' these are luminous intrusions. ... Pound saw in the convergent gestures to the right of the character rays entering a focus, and did not care that such an etymology was impossible, before there were lenses. Add 口, a word, and we have 試, Mathews 381, a word perfected, hence sincere, true, honest: but in Pound's world of light-philosophers 'the sun's lance coming to rest on the precise spot verbally.'"

5. POUND, Confucius, op.cit., 'Chung Yung,' p.167.

6. Ibid., p.173.

7. FINGARETTE, Confucius, op.cit., p.15: "Once we are aware of the ceremonial or performative kinds of functions of language, the original texts begin to read differently."

8. Ibid., pp.13-15.

9. KENNER, Pound Era, op.cit., p.13.

10. Ibid.

11. Cf. FINGARETTE, Confucius, op.cit., Chapter 4, 'Traditionalist Or Visionary?'.

12. POUND, Canto 96, p.655.

13. Cf. R. PANIKKAR, 'Silence & The Word, The Smile of The Buddha' Myth, Faith and Hermeneutics, op.cit., pp. 257-276.

14. FINGARETTE, Confucius, op.cit., Chapter 4. Cf. also W. Taylor STEVENSON, History as Myth, New York (Seabury) 1969, one of the earliest studies to stress this theme.

15. A good overview of the period is provided by W.-C. LIU, A Short History of Confucian Philosophy (Abridged), New York (Dell) 1955.

16. As it is by Achilles FANG in his 'Note On the Stone Classics,' which prefaces POUND's Confucius, op.cit, pp.11-15. It should however be added that Pound probably MISconstrued Buddhism and Hinduism quite as thoroughly as he really did manage to understand the Confucian tradition. He generally sees in these great traditions little more than negativism, vacuity and, in the case of Buddhist "beggars," laziness. He also seems to have a bone to pick with Taoism -- "and taozers turn out to chase devils" (Canto 99) -- and fails to notice the extent to which his own understanding of Confucius bears a markedly Taoist stamp. Cf. the discussion of the "Seven Lakes Canto" (XLIX) in PEARLMAN, The Barb of Time, op.cit., pp.304-5.

17. POUND, Canto 99, p.697.

18. See EXHIBIT, 'Tsze Tsze's Third Thesis,' at the end of this chapter. Pound renders CHU HSI's 'Preface' to the Chung Yung; from which (POUND, Confucius, op.cit., p.97):

"My master the philosopher Ch'eng says: the word <u>chung</u> signifies what is bent neither to one side nor to the other. The word <u>yung</u> signifies unchanging. What exists plum in the middle is the just process [<u>Tao</u>] of the universe, and that which never wavers or wobbles is the calm principle operant in its mode of action.

"...At its start the book speaks of the one principle, it then spreads into a discussion of things in general, and concludes by uniting all this in the one principle. Spread it out and its arrows reach to the six ends of the universe, zenith and nadir; fold it again and it withdraws to serve you in secret as faithful minister."

19. Cf. also R. PANIKKAR, <u>El Silencio Del Dios</u>, Madrid (Tiempo al tiempo) 1970, III 'La Hermeneutica.'

20. POUND, <u>Confucius</u>, op.cit., 'Chung Yung,' p.187. It is worth noting that <u>T'ien</u> --"Heaven" --is a term really quite untranslatable as "Spirit," or "God," or "Supreme Being," or even "Paradise." It is much more concrete than any of these. One is put in mind of Hölderlin's awareness of divinity as "the face of the sky."

21. POUND, Canto 85, p.552.

22. POUND, Canto LXXIV, p.425.

*EXHIBIT: 'Tsze Tsze's Third Thesis,' excerpted from POUND, <u>Confucius</u>, op.cit., pp.171-183.

C/ Theological Transparencies

* KENNER, Pound Era, op.cit., p.350.

** Namely the Pisan Cantos through and including Drafts & Fragments.

7 The Poetic Vocation

a/ The Poet's Calling

1. POUND, Canto 99, p.707. Cf. also ibid.: "Thru the ten voices of the tradition/ the land has been ploughed..."

2. A. UPWARD, The Divine Mystery, op.cit., Chapter 1.

3. M. ELIADE, Shamanism, op.cit. Note especially Chapters I 'Shamanism & Mystical Vision,' II 'Initiatory Sickness & Dreams,' III 'Obtaining Shamanic Powers,' and IV 'Shamanic Initiation.'

4. Cf. M. ELIADE, The Sacred & the Profane, New York, (Harcourt, Brace & World) 1959. Although it should be noted that Eliade himself may be the most formidable example of shamanism in the modern academic world.

5. J. NEIHARDT, Black Elk Speaks, Lincoln (Univ. of Nebraska Press) 1961; especially Chapter II, 'The Great Vision,' pp.20-47.

6. C. CASTENADA, e.g., Tales of Power, New York (Simon & Schuster) 1974. Cf. also Joan HALIFAX, Shamanic Voices, New York (Dutton) 1979, for an excellent survey of shamanic narratives.

7. ELIADE's Shamanism, op.cit., is primarily what sparked the interest, followed by such intriguing tracts as E.A.S. BUTTERWORTH, The Tree At the Navel of the Earth, op.cit. Much work in this area has been done in Amerindian studies, beginning with classic compendia like Gladys A. REICHARD's study of sandpaintings and attendant shamanic rites in Navajo Religion, A Study of Symbolism, New York (Bollingen) 1963. Also cf. G. de SANTILLANA & H. von DECHEND, Hamlet's Mill, Boston (Godine) 1977, e.g., Chapter VIII, 'Shamans and Smiths,' p.113 et seq., and Joseph CAMPBELL's Masks of God volume on "Primitive Religions," New York (Viking) 1959.

8. Cf. ELIADE, Shamanism, op.cit., Chapter VIII, 'Shamanism & Cosmology.'

9. One notable attempt at assimilation which also attests to the difficulties involved, is Stephen LARSEN's intriguing book, The Shaman's Doorway, New York (Harper & Row) 1976.

10. Cf. S.R. HOPPER, 'Le Cri de Merlin! Or Interpretation and the Metalogical,' Anagogic Qualities of Literature, op.cit., p.10: "The contemporary literary artist participates radically, even agonistically, in the deep revision of Western consciousness that is going on about us. He is thrust, by the nature of his calling, into that reasonating void between that which has ceased to be and that which is not yet." Cf. also M. HEIDEGGER's discussion of Rilke in 'What Are Poets For...?,' Poetry, Language, Thought, op.cit., pp.91-142.

11. POUND, Canto 93, p.632.

b/ The Poets Who Call

12. Langue, not langage.

13. Logan Pearsall SMITH, The English Language, London (Oxford) 1966, Chapter 1, 'The Origin of the English Language,' p.11: "When the early physicists became aware of forces they could not understand, they turned to escape their difficulty by personifying the laws of nature and invoking 'spirits' that controlled material phenomena. The student of language, in the presence of the mysterious power which creates and changes language, has been compelled to adopt this medieval procedure, and has vaguely defined, by the name 'the Genius of the Language,' the power that guides and controls its progress." Cf. Also Lewis THOMAS, Lives of A Cell; Notes of a Biology Watcher, New York (Viking) 1974, especially the chapter 'Living Language,' pp. 156-64, for an attempt to reconcile the language of genetics and the genetics of language. Cf. Also KENNER, Pound Era, op.cit., p. 490.

14. Cf. M. HEIDEGGER, 'Poetically Man Dwells,' Poetry, Language, Thought, op.cit., p.215: "Mans acts as if he were the shaper and master of language, while it is language which remains mistress of man. ... For in fact it is language that speaks. Man begins speaking and man only speaks to the extent that he responds to, that he corresponds with language, and only insofar as he hears language addressing, concurring with him."

15. Friedrich HÖLDERLIN, 'Celebration of Peace,' Michael Hamburger, trans., Ann Arbor (Univ. of Michigan Press) 1967, p.438. Cited by HEIDEGGER often, e.g., in 'The Way to Language,' On the Way to Language, op.cit., p.135.

16. Aliter, for our topic, "song": canto.

17. Cf. George STEINER, 'Understanding as Translation,' in After Babel, Aspects of Language and Translation, op.cit., pp.1-48.

18. In his discussion of Canto I; KENNER, Pound Era, op.cit., pp.349-55.

19. Cf., e.g., KENNER, Pound Era, op.cit., p.486: "There are eerie moments in the Pisan Cantos when he suddenly becomes some other." And not only in the Pisan Cantos...

20. Cf. Richmond LATTIMORE, The Odyssey of Homer, A Modern Translation, op.cit., Book XI, pp.168-184.

21. As Pound returned to the USA over water in 1945, under indictment for treason.

22. Cf. KENNER, Pound Era, op.cit., p.231.

23. Cf., e.g., J.N. EDWARDS & W.V. VASSE, The Annotated Index to the Cantos I - LXXXIV, Berkeley (UC Press) 1957.

c/ The Call

24. Others, Hugh Kenner and Donald Davie chief among them, have detailed these connections in greater detail than would serve our purposes here. The coherence of the whole, however, still remains elusive for most readers of Pound.

25. POUND, Spirit of Romance, op.cit., p.88.

26. Cf. KENNER, Pound Era., op.cit., 'The Cage,' pp.460-95 for elucidation, particularly of her most startling apparition in Canto LXXXI: "There came new subtlety of eyes into my tent."

27. Here it may be worthwhile to refer the reader to Erich NEUMANN, The Great Mother, New York (Bollingen) 1955, for a comprehensive analysis of the archetype of the feminine, built on a Jungian basis from materials collected in the Eranos Library for Symbolic Research, Zurich. Part I is especially instructive as to the various -- and often apparently contradictory -- "faces" or "characters" of the Great Goddess. Cf. also C.G. JUNG & K. KERENYI, Essays on a Science of Mythology, New York (Bollingen) 1949, Part II (Kerenyi) 'Koré,' and Part IV (Jung) 'Psychological Aspects of the Koré.'

28. Cf. POUND, 'Cavalcanti,' Translations, op.cit.

29. Cf. POUND, 'Arnaut Daniel,' Translations, op.cit., and the interpolated chapter 'Psychology & Troubadors' in Spirit of Romance, op.cit.

30. The love mysticism of Islamic esoterism and some of its ramifications for medieval Christianity are splendidly explicated in Henry CORBIN, Creative Imagination in the Sufism of Ibn 'Arabi, Ralph Manheim,

trans., New York (Bollingen) 1969. Cf. also R.A.
NICHOLSON, trans., The Tarjumán Al-Ashwáq (Interpreter
of Ardent Desires) by Muhi'ddin Ibn Al-'Arabi, London
(Royal Asiatic Society) 1911.

31. Cf. Robert GRAVES, The White Goddess, A Historical
Grammar of Poetic Myth, New York (Farrar, Strauss &
Giroux) 1948, particularly Chapter XXII, 'The Triple
Muse' for the Gaelic and Celtic underpinnings of the
flowering of mystical love poems in medieval Europe.

32. Indeed, RICHARD OF ST. VICTOR has left us Benjamin
Major, a mystical itinerary based in part on St.
Deny's "celestial hierarchy," in which the Soul travels to meet its Beloved. Pound apparently knew this
work as well as he knew St. Denys and Erigena.

33. POUND, 'Psychology & Troubadors,' Spirit of Romance, op.cit., pp.96-7.

34. The nature of the creative act, its very dynamism,
is sacrifice. Cf. R. PANIKKAR, 'The Originating Fault
or Creative Immolation; The Myth of Prajāpati,' Myth,
Faith & Hermeneutics, op.cit. pp.65-95.

35. POUND, Translations, op.cit., p.19.

36. Dante ALIGHIERI, The New Life, (Vita Nuova), Wm.
Anderson trans., Baltimore (Penguin) 1964, p.110.

37. POUND, Spirit of Romance, op.cit., p.97.

38. POUND, Canto LXXVI, p.457.

39. POUND, CANTO LXXX, P.493.

40. POUND, 'Calvalcanti,' Translations, op.cit., p.18.

41. For oblique corroboration, cf. PEARLMAN, Barb of
Time, op.cit., p.243: "Pound projects his own
spiritual journey onto the motions of stars and
planets which more and more come to symbolize the
poet's progress toward self-renewal." In Pearlman's
insightful study, linear, historical time is "the
evil," the destroyer, while circular, rhythmic, recurrent time comes to be defined as love, the pattern by
which the whole coheres.

THE SETTING;
An Interpolation

*EXCERPT FROM W.B. YEATS, A Vision, op.cit., pp.3-5.

8 The Music of the Spheres

1. POUND, Impact; Essays on Ignorance and the Decline of American Civilization, Noel STOCK, ed., Chicago (Henry Regnery) 1960, p.15.

a/ Distinctions in Clarity

2. "Distinctions in clarity": cheng ming; cf. Chapter 6.

3. "Subject-rhyme" is a phrase originating with Hugh Kenner; cf. KENNER, Pound Era, op.cit., e.g., P.423. It has by now become more or less common coin in the "Pound industry."

4. This anecdote, related to me some time ago by conversation with Prof. Kenner, echoes the longstanding Poundian dictum: "The natural object is always the adequate symbol," POUND, 'Credo,' in 'A Retrospect' (Pavannes & Divagations, 1918), Literary Essays, op.cit., p.9.

5. POUND, Canto 104, p.742.

6. POUND, Canto 93, p. 631.

7. Ibid., p.632.

8. POUND, from 'Notes for Canto CXVII et seq., p.802.

9. POUND, Canto CXVI, p.796.

10. Ibid., p.797.

11. For example, A. ALVAREZ, in 'Craft and Morals,' Ezra Pound, Perspectives: Essays in Honor of his Eightieth Birthday, Noel STOCK, ed., Chicago (Henry Regnery) 1965, has this to say about the coherence of The Cantos (p.654): "The work has the hustle of artistic life, but not its inevitability. It is full of names, figures and action; but the abiding central life of the artist judging and ordering the details, creating them in his own coherence, is not there."

12. Noel STOCK, Poet in Exile: Ezra Pound, New York

(Barnes & Noble) 1964, p.122: "He begins to insert...
lines which cannot bear the weight of meaning he
intends... the meaning of the whole work becomes no
clearer as he passes Canto 50, and then Canto 70, and
actually begins to recede after he passes into the
Rock-Drill section (Cantos 85-95)... the job of giving
a major form to such a vast undertaking is beyond him,
and when cracks begin to show he tries to fill them
with hasty and inferior material." Cf. also the final
chapter or two of STOCK, The Life of Ezra Pound,
op.cit., for more of the same.

13. This was actually Kenner's final remark in the
last lecture he delivered on Pound's Cantos at the
University of California, Santa Barbara, after more
than 20 years of teaching Pound there. Yet Kenner, in
contrast to Stock et al., has always seen something of
this overall coherence. From his first book on Pound,
The Poetry of Ezra Pound, New York (New Directions)
1951, p.300: "It was Pound's discovery that the logical end of conscientious rendering was an epic without
(in the usual sense) a plot... In the Cantos the
place of a plot is taken by interlocking large-scale
rhythms of recurrence."

14. G.P. ELLIOTT, 'Poet of Many Voices,' in W. SUTTON,
ed., Ezra Pound: A Collection of Critical Essays, New
Jersey (Prentice-Hall) 1963, p.277.

15. Cf. POUND, Guide to Kulchur, op.cit., Chapter 7
'Great Bass: Part One' and Chapter 42 'Great Bass:
Part Two.'

16. There is a Poundian terminology almost adaptable
to our purposes here, but perhaps over-complex; cf.
the discussion of phanopoeia, melopoeia and logopoeia
under the rubric 'Language' in 'How to Read,' Literary
Essays, op.cit., p.25.

17. In the sense of Hans-Georg GADAMER's program of a
"universal hermeneutics" in Part III of his Truth and
Method, op.cit., 'The Ontological Shift of Hermeneutics Guided by Language.' (Warheit und Methode,
Tubingen, 1960.)

18. Cf. PEARLMAN, Barb of Time, op.cit., p.34: "Very
little in life is more tedious than reading through
discussions of The Cantos constructed on the mechanical principle of canto-by-canto explication... such
studies unconsciously confess to an absence of any

perception of over-all structure in The Cantos -- a failure to see the wood for the trees."

19. POUND, Women of Trachis (Sophocles' Trachinae), New York (New Directions) 1957, p.50. In the text of his translation Pound renders the line cited:

"...what

SPLENDOUR,

IT ALL COHERES."

and his footnote to it begins: "This is the key phrase, for which the play exists..."

20. KENNER, Pound Era, op.cit., p.168.

21. Ibid.

22. KENNER, Bucky, A Guided Tour of Buckminster Fuller, New York (Wm. Morrow) 1973, Chapter 1 refers to Kenner's work on Pound: "Bucky might have told me I was looking for a Coordinate System. In a book I wrote about Pound in 1949 [Poetry of Ezra Pound] I did manage a couple of intuitive axioms. One was that the same law governs the whole and the parts. If you can understand how a man fits a sentence together, you have a model for his way of building larger units. That was one glimpse of continuity."(p.6) ...
"His talk (late 1967) solved for me, that week, a book called The Pound Era I had been trying to think out for years and was suddenly able to start writing." (p.11)

23. I.e., Fuller. Cf. KENNER's famous example of the knot slipped rope to rope in the Chapter 'Knot & Vortex' (p.145 et seq.) in The Pound Era, op.cit. In Bucky, op.cit., he provides instructions for building a tensegrity icosa from dowelling and wires.

b/ The Celestial Hierarchies

24. Cf. R. PANIKKAR, 'Philosophy & Revolution; Text, Context & Texture,' Philosophy East & West, Vol.3, July 1973, pp.315-22.

25. KENNER article in the last LOOK Magazine (Fall, 1972) in which he mentions both Pound and Fuller.

26. Cf., e.g., lines like: "but our job to build light, said Ocellus," Canto 98, p.684. One perfectly coherent way to read the later Cantos is to see the whole of it as Pound saw Dante's Paradiso -- as a single elaborated metaphor on the theme of LIGHT. Light radiates out from centers in spherical waves, the behavior and properties of which are modelled and mapped by Fuller's geodesic figures. In Canto LXXIV and elsewhere, Pound quotes Scotus Erigena to make his point: "Omnia quae sunt sunt lumina," "all things that are are lights."

27. Cf. Walter B. MICHAEL's informative short article 'Pound and Erigena' in Paideuma, Vol.1, No.1 (Spring/ Summer 1972).

28. That of St. Denys. Cf. Maurice De GANDILLAC, Oeuvres Complètes du Pseudo-Denys L'Aréopagite, Paris (Aubier) 1943, 'La Hiérarchie Céleste,' pp.185-244.

29. Cf. KENNER, Pound Era, op.cit., p.246: "...Pound was immersed in the orchestration of the new sensibility, decisive and blocked and faceted, a vortex of vortices, in touch with Li Po and Provence and Chou bronzes and Flaubert and Feng Shui, the Chinese geomancer's art of detecting the rhymes and unrhymes of the local cosmos. Unimpeded by fussy 'tradition,' virtù free as light in space could intersect (with precision, with immediacy) any tradition it chose." Add to this Kenner's observation that "...vortices intersect like geodesics" and you have the key to our presentation in this chapter and the next.

30. Cf. R.B. FULLER & E.J. APPLEWHITE, Synergetics, Explorations in the Geometry of Thinking, op.cit., e.g., 516.00 'Frequency Modulation,': "Synergetics is the first to introduce the time dimension integrally as the frequency of systems... (i.e.) the modular subdividing of the primitive, metaphysical, timeless systems." Three quite crucial instances of such "primitive, metaphysical, timeless" polyhedra will be presented in the Illustrations. Cf. Synergetics for frequency extrapolations, the "spheres within spheres" of shell growth in closest packing of spheres, for example.

31. From the 'Weekly Review' in a Philadelphia newspaper, 12 December 1909: "Mr. Pound is now delivering a course of lectures at the London Polytechnic on Medieval Literature and we are jealous of the fact

that England should have discovered and honoured his genius rather than his own native America, but we are duly proud of him as a son of Pennsylvania." Cited in STOCK, Life of Ezra Pound, op.cit., p.79.

32. Laurence Binyon's English translation of The Divine Comedy is available in The Portable Dante, New York (Viking) 1952. The story of Pound's association with Binyon is a long and fascinating one. Some highlights:

1908   Pound meets Binyon, attends his lecture in London on 'Oriental & European Art,' which he pronouces "intensely interesting."

1914   BLAST carries a short piece by Pound on Binyon, in which Pound quotes from Binyon's 'Flight of the Dragon.' A sample:

> "Art is not an adjunct to existence, a reproduction of the actual." (p.19)
> "FOR INDEED IT IS NOT ESSENTIAL THAT THE SUBJECT-MATTER SHOULD REPRESENT OR BE LIKE ANYTHING IN NATURE; ONLY IT MUST BE ALIVE WITH A RHYTHMIC VITALITY OF ITS OWN." (p.21)

1934   Criterion publishes Pound's 'Hell' (Literary Essary, op.cit., p.201 et seq.), in which he recommends that Binyon's Inferno replace the Temple Edition as the authoritative introduction to Dante in English. Pound writes:

> "Fools have their uses, and had it not been for the professional pomp of Mr. Wubb or whatever his name is, I might not have found the volume. [Binyon's Inferno.] Mr. Wubb leapt upon Binyon's opening traid of lines and managed to display such complete ignorance of the nature of Dantescan verse, and at the same time so thoroughly indicated at least one virtue of Binyon's work that I was aroused to wonder if the venerable Binyon had been able to keep on at that pace. ... The venerable Binyon has, I am glad to say, produced the most interesting English version of Dante I have seen or expect to see..."
> (Criterion, April 1934)

1938　An　enormously　detailed　correspondence
　　　ensues　between　Pound　and　Binyon　--　line　by
　　　line,　word　by　word　--　on　the　Purgatorio.
　　　Pound　writes　Binyon:　　"I　am　not　writing　a
　　　critique,　I　am　going　over　the　text　with　a
　　　microscope."
　　　(Letters　343,　344,　346-9,　POUND,　Letters
　　　of,　D.D.　PAIGE,　ed.,　op.cit.)

The　final　correspondence　is　dated　12　May　1938,
from　Pound　in　Rapallo:

　　　"And　now,　Boss,　you　get　RIGHT　ALONG　with
　　　that　Paradiso　as　soon　as　you've　stacked　up
　　　the　dinner　dishes.　Why　don't　the　twins
　　　[i.e.　EP　&　LB]　do　some　work?
　　　"Bonzai,　alaila."　(Letter　349,　Letters,
　　　p.318)

　　　Then　World　War　II　intervened.　But　Pound　had
apparently　done　his　homework　on　Dantescan　minutiae,
appropriately　enough　in　the　Purgatorio.　Binyon　completed　his　translation　of　the　Paradiso　and　died　in
1943.　After　the　war　Pound,　by　contrast,　was　indicted
for　treason　and　confined　to　a　mental　ward.　And　yet　he
also　believed　he　was　carrying　out　the　projected
Paradiso.

33.　Cf.　Canto　XXVIII,　130-9,　'Paradiso,'　BINYON
Trans.,　Portable　Dante,　op.cit.,　pp.516-17,　where
Dante　vindicates　Dionysus'　scheme　over　that　of　Gregory
of　Nyssa.　Beatrice　is　speaking:

"Dionysus　set　himself　so　ardently
　　　to　fix　upon　these　orders　his　regard,
　　　He　named　them　and　distinguished　them　as　I.
But　Gregory　parted　from　him　afterward,
　　　Though　at　himself　he　smiled　when　all　things　were
　　　In　heaven　to　his　enlightened　eyes　unbarred.
And　if　on　earth　a　mortal　could　declare
　　　A　truth　so　secret,　be　not　stupefied;
　　　For　he　imparted　it　who　saw　it　here
With　much　of　truth　about　these　gyres　beside."

34.　Cf.　AVICENNA,　La　Récit　de　Hayy　Ibn　Yāqzan,　A.M.
GOICHON,　trans.,　Paris　(Desclée　de　Broumer)　1959,
e.g.,　Chapitre　IX,　'Le　Voyage　de　L'Ame　Dans　Le　Monde
Des　Intelligibles.'

35.　Cf.　M.　De　GANDILLAC,　Oeuvres　Complétes　du　Pseudo-

Denys L'Aréopagite, op.cit., pp.186-7 (speaking of "les saintes initiateurs qui ont primitivement réglé nos rites" --): "Voulant, dans leur amour pour notre humanité, nous déifier à la mesure de nos forces en nous révélent les célestes hiérarchies et en permettant à notre proper hiérarchie de les imiter, autant que le peut une institution humaine, afin qu'elle entre en collégialité avec ce sacerdoce angelique dont la forme est divine, nos initiateurs ont dû representer par des images sensibles, à travers les saintes allegories que rapportent les Ecritures, de façon à nous élever spirituellement du sensible à l'intelligible et des images sacrées et symbolique aux cimes des hiérarchies célestes."

36. Cf. ELIADE, Shamanism, op.cit., Chapter VIII.

37. St. Denys' (pseudo-Dionysus') term for the Trinity is curious: he calls it the Thearchy. Thus the arché of the theos is this triangulation, which pervades not only everything St. Denys wrote, but is at the root of Dante's terza rima (3-line stanzas) as well as his tripartite Commedia itself. Cf. also R. PANIKKAR's "re-vision" of the Christian Trinity in the light of the Hindu tradition(s) in The Trinity and the Religious Experience of Man, London (Darton, Longman & Todd)/New York (Orbis) 1973. Panikkar's work may well be the most powerful thinking through of the trinitarian vision in about 700 years.

38. Cf. W.B. MICHAELS, 'Pound & Erigena,' Paideuma, op.cit.

39. Cf. R.B. FULLER & E.J. APPLEWHITE, Synergetics, op.cit., 430.00 'Vector Equilibrium.'

40. Cheng ming; cf. our Chapter 6.

41. "Ephemeralization": R.B. Fuller's term for "doing more and more with less and less."

42. Cf. 'The Myths of Paradise,' Part I, Chapter 1 of this study.

43. D.D. PEARLMAN, The Barb of Time, op.cit., p.20. For this "dimension of stillness," vide. the last lines of POUND, Cantos XLVII and XLIX.

44. POUND, Guide to Kulchur, op.cit., 'Dichten: condensare.' Cf. also KENNER, Pound Era, op.cit., p.61: "In the summer of 1916 he had reduced 'the whole art,'

for Iris Barry's benefit, to:
  '<u>a</u>. concision, or style, or saying what you
      mean in the fewest and clearest words.
   <u>b</u>. the actual necessity for creating or
      constructing something; of presenting
      an image, or enough images of concrete
      things arranged to stir the reader.'"

45. From POUND's 'Note' to his translation of the
Analects, Confucius, op.cit., p.194.

46. Just so, no "point" Pound makes in The Cantos is
wholly accessible -- or sometimes even intelligible --
without reference to the larger whole. This should by
now be a truism.

47. "Some texts come into the world needing foot-
notes," Hugh KENNER, 'A Calithumpian Life,' review of
a biography of Samuel Beckett in Saturday Review,
August, 1978.

48. I employ this term "foci of attention" for two
reasons: Hugh KENNER, in his glossary to Bucky
(op.cit., pp.317-20) glosses "Event: A unit of attention, characterized by the biblical 'It came to
pass.'" And, secondly, Jane Ellen Harrison, in the
first chapter of her classic Themis (London, 1912),
defines "Sanctities: foci of attention." It seems to
me that the congruence of these two definitions more
closely comes to grips with Pound's "nodes" than
either taken alone.

49. J. WILHELM, The Later Cantos of Ezra Pound, New
York (Walker & Walker) 1977, p.46.

50. By no means does the existence of references imply
that Pound is "copying" or "imitating" Dante. He
intends, as always, to "make it new." One important
deviation is that Pound "could not swallow" Aquinas.
In 1934 he wrote: "As to the form of The Cantos: All
I can say or pray is: wait till it's there. I mean
wait till I get 'em written and then if it don't show,
I will start exegesis. I haven't an Aquinas-map;
Aquinas not valid now." From D.D. PEARLMAN, Barb of
Time, op.cit., p.32. But strip the "form" of Dante's
Paradiso of Aquinas, and what remains is mainly the
nine heavens (the intelligences of St. Denys) crossed
with the "logical astrology" Pound refers to in the
Introduction to his 'Cavalcanti' (Translations, op.cit.,
loc.cit.), plus a large helping of local politics. And
Beatrice.

51. Cf. KENNER's "mapping" of the early Cantos (I-XVI) in The Pound Era, op.cit., pp.416-17. Such an index can be of enormous help, but in the final analysis every serious reader of Pound marks out for him/herself an itinerary, notable landmarks, points of interest, etc., according to their own lights and blind spots.

Counterpoint: Pound on Harmony

* POUND, Antheil, or The Treatise on Harmony, London (Peter Owen Ltd.) 1962, reprint of original edition of 40 copies published by Three Mountains Press, Paris, 1927, by Covici.

** Cf. POUND, Introduction to 'Cavalcanti,' Translations, op.cit., loc.cit.

*** Cf. POUND, 'Arnold Dolmetsch' (Pavannes & Divagations, 1918) and 'Vers Libre & Arnold Dolmetsch' (also 1918) in Literary Essays, op.cit., pp.431-40. Dolmetsch is best known for his Interpretation of the Music of the XVIIth and XVIIIth Centuries, New York (W.H. Gray & Co.), and for bringing the recorder back into common usage. Pound kept a handmade Dolmetsch clavichord until the end of his life. In the latter article, Pound begins by stating outright: "Poetry is a composition of words set to music." In the former article, after his first hearing of Dolmetsch's recorder, Pound wrote: "I have seen the God Pan..."

9 The Divine Diaphany

1. POUND, 'Note' to Analects trans., Confucius, op.cit., loc.cit.

2. Periplus: "a sailing round," a circumnavigation. POUND renders it "periplum" in the Pisan Cantos; it seems there to indicate places where the seafarer "touches ground."

3. I will be employing Binyon's Divine Comedy, since it is presumably the one with which Pound was most familiar, apart from the original, while composing the later Cantos. For purposes of cross-reference, a serviceable bilingual text is John D. SINCLAIR, The Divine Comedy of Dante Alighieri: III 'Paradiso,' New York (Oxford) 1939. This text, in three volumes, seems to have replaced the Temple Edition as a favorite of college professors nowadays. Sinclair, however, badly misconstrues the number of heavens -- he counts ten, having tossed the Empyrean into the same lot as the nine -- a sin against the spirit of St. Denys which may be indicative of other weaknesses.

4. Cf. R.B. FULLER & E.J. APPLEWHITE, Synergetics, op.cit., 'Introduction: The Wellspring of Reality,' p.xxvi: "The word generalization in literature usually means covering too much territory too thinly to be persuasive, let alone convincing. In science, however, a generalization means a principle that has been found to hold true in every special case."
Cf. also KENNER, Pound Era, op.cit., p.162: "Buckminster Fuller adduces a general law:
   'Heisenberg said that observation alters the phenomenon observed. T.S. Eliot said that studying history alters history. Ezra Pound said that thinking in general alters what is thought about. Pound's formulation is the most general, and I think it's the earliest.'
[Kenner continues:] "Where, when, in what connection had Pound said that? Fuller couldn't remember, he'd read it long ago; it would take weeks to find it. No matter: such a self-interfering pattern does not derive its power from its credentials. To think of Pound in that way alters Pound."

5. POUND, Spirit of Romance, op.cit., p.127. Cf. also the passage on geometry in POUND, Gaudier-Brzeska, op.cit, pp.90-2. It is my feeling that Pound's own approach to Dante provides a more useful key to Pound's later Cantos than simply chalking it all up to

the techniques of collage, as Marjorie Perloff suggests in her recent book, The Poetics of Indeterminacy:
From Rimbaud to Cage, New Jersey (Princeton) 1982.
Certainly collage techniques are employed, but is this
the principle by which the whole coheres?

Hymns & Spheres

The First Sphere

6. M. de GANDILLAC, Pseudo-Denys, op.cit., 'La
Hiérarchie Céleste,' loc.cit., Chapitre VI: 'Quel est
le premier ordre des essences célestes, quel l'ordre
moyen, quel l'ordre inferieur,' pp.205-6.

7. BINYON, trans., 'The Divine Comedy,' Portable
Dante, op.cit., loc.cit., 'Paradiso,' Cantos I-V.

8. POUND, Pisan Cantos, pp.423-540.

9. Canto LXXIV, p.443. It is noteworthy that the
Cytherean Venus (more properly of the third sphere,
but undoubtedly resplendent as the morning and evening
star in the Pisan twilight) makes her appearance
often. Above all, it is "the Beloved," Pound's mute
Beatrice, who visits and consoles him in the cage.
Cf. also D.D. CARNE-ROSS, 'The Music of a Lost
Dynasty; Pound in the Classroom,' Boston University
Journal, Winter 1972, p.31: "There is a lot of lunar
poetry in the Pisans."

10. "Zeus lies in Ceres' bosom" is the first line of
POUND, Canto LXXXI; the "Elysium" line occurs later in
the same Canto, p.521. Cf. also KENNER, Pound Era,
op.cit., 'The Cage,' pp.488-540, which includes the
finest and most understanding treatment of Canto
LXXXI: "Is there another passage in literature that
can number among the protagonists in its drama the
meter itself?" (p.493)

11. POUND, Canto LXXIX, p.488.

12. POUND, Canto LXXXI, p.519.

13. POUND, Canto LXXIV, p.443.

14. POUND, Canto LXXIV, p.438.

The Second Sphere

15. DANTE, 'Paradiso,' Cantos V-VII, Divine Comedy, op.cit.

16. POUND, Cantos 85-95, pp.543-604.

17. POUND, Canto 85, p.543.

18. DANTE, 'Paradiso,' Canto VI, Divine Comedy, op.cit.

19. POUND, The Confucian Odes, New York (New Directions) 1954.

20. Cf. KENNER, Gnomon, for an essay on this topic.

The Third Sphere

21. DANTE, 'Paradiso,' Cantos VIII-IX, Divine Comedy, op.cit.

22. POUND, Cantos 90-93, pp.605-32.

23. POUND, Canto 90, final line, p.609. The quotation from Richard of St. Victor which accompanies this is worth noting in full, along with Pound's translation of it in the text of Canto 90:

(Richard:)
Animus humanus amor non est,
sed ab ipso amor procedit, et
ideo seipso non diligit, sed amore
qui seipso procedit.
(p.605)

(Pound:)
[The human soul is]
Not love but that love flows from it
ex animo
& cannot ergo delight in itself
but only in the love flowing from it.
UBI AMOR IBI OCULUS EST.   (p.609)

24. POUND, Canto 91, p.610.

25. A Pound "ideogram" -- Ra (Egyptian God of the sun) and Set (his eternal adversary, the darkness) combined in the "Princess Ra-Set," whose "golden sun boat" (p.612) moves the hard way, "by oar not by sail." Nevertheless, "A man's paradise is his good nature" -- Pound soon adds in the voice and hieroglyphics of the Egyptian poet Kati (p.623).

26. The quotation is from DANTE 'Paradiso,' Canto XXVI, line 34: "It is fitting that what moves the mind is love." Cf. also POUND, Canto LXXXI: "What thou lov'st well remains."

27. ichor: The stuff that flows in the veins of God (i.e. amor, love). A powerful fusion of matrices -- the Greek and the Tuscan -- in two words.

28. POUND, Canto 91, p.611.

The Fourth Sphere

29. DANTE, 'Paradiso,' Cantos X-XII, Divine Comedy, op.cit.

30. POUND, Cantos 94-5, pp.633-47.

31. POUND, Canto 94, p.635: "Let the light pour, that is, toward sinceritas/ of the word/ comprehensive..."

32. POUND, Canto 94, p.642.

33. Ibid., P.638. The final line is from Philostratus' account of the travels of Apollonius of Tyana; cf. below.

34. F.C. CONYBEARE, Philostratus' Life of Apollonius of Tyana, New York (Macmillan) 1912.

35. Except Norman O. Brown, whom I have to thank for putting me on the track of it...

36. Apollonius Rhodius.

37. POUND, Canto 94, p.637; erota iskei concerns the universe's "love for itself," discussed in the passage cited below. It is perhaps also a pun: "and that the universe is alive/ by love possessed." Cf. also Dante's final lines in Il Paradiso, "the love that moves the sun and other stars," Divine Comedy, op.cit., p.544.

38. CONYBEARE, Philostratus' Life of Apollonius of Tyana, op.cit., Book III, p.309. A final note from this extraordinarily rich volume would be to cite, a propos of Ezra Pound, Apollonius' recommendation to the priest of a local temple (p.27) that he trust the Gods enough to make only the following prayer: "O ye gods, grant unto us that which we deserve." This has come to be known as "The Prayer of Apollonius."

The Fifth Sphere

39. DANTE, 'Paradiso,' Cantos XIV-XVII, Divine Comedy, op.cit.

40. POUND, Cantos 96-98, pp.651-693.

41. POUND, Canto 97, p.676(-79).

42. Ibid., p.668.

43. POUND also seems to have recognized the problem. In Canto 96 (p.659) he justifies his approach in a curious aside: "If we never write anything save what is already understood, the field of understanding will never be extended. One demands the right, now and again, to write for a few people with special interests and whose curiosity reaches into greater detail."

44. POUND, Canto 97, p.676. The triple-pillared temple is apparently an artifact of Pound's own.

The Sixth Sphere

45. DANTE, 'Paradiso,' Cantos XVIII-XX, Divine Comedy, op.cit.

46. POUND, Cantos 99-105, pp.694-751.

47. Prepared for in Canto 98, rendered in Canto 99, the Edict of the Emperor Iong Cheng (cf. Canto XLI). Every line of Canto 99 is rich and worthy of more explication than would be appropriate here. Pound puts himself in the position of one "Wang, Commissioner of Salt Works," who "carried the sense" of the Emperor's Edict down to the people (cf. Canto 98).

48. POUND, Canto 99, p.695.

49. Ibid., p.705.

50. Cf. POUND's 'Foreword' to The Selected Essays of Ezra Pound, 1909-1965, op.cit., p.6: "re USURY: I was out of focus, taking a symptom for a cause. The cause is AVARICE. (Venice, 4th July, 1972)"

51. Available on Caedmon Records.

52. POUND, Canto 98, p.693 and elsewhere.

53. POUND, Canto 99, p.698.

54. Ibid., p.699.

55. Ibid., p.702.

56. Ibid. p.712.

The Seventh Sphere

57. St. Denys describes the quality of the first three
intelligences, moving outward from the Thearchy, as a
process of (1) Purification (Seraphim), (2) Illumination (Cherubim) and (3) Perfection (Thrones). Cf.
GANDILLAC, Pseudo-Denys, op.cit., Chapitre X: 'Reca-
pitulation et conclusion concernant la bonne ordonnance
des hiérarchies angéliques,' pp.221-3.

58. DANTE, 'Paradiso,' Canto XXI, Divine Comedy,
op.cit.

59. POUND, Cantos 106-109, pp.752-74. Cantos 107-109
resemble Cantos 100-105 in density and opacity. Canto
106 is a distinct change in tone.

60. POUND, Canto 106, p.752.

61. Ibid., p. 754.

62. Ibid., p.755.

63. DANTE, 'Paradiso,' Divine Comedy, op.cit., Canto
IX, line 61: "Above are Mirrors -- Thrones ye call
thcm --".

64. POUND, Canto 109, p.774:
      "Le chapeau melon de St. Pierre"
Decadence of the Church manifest in its architecture,
and --
      "You in the dinghy (piccioletta) astern there!"
-- Charon's question to Dante as they cross Styx;
"What are you, a live man, doing here in the world of
the dead?" Indeed.

65. Cf. KENNER, Pound Era, op.cit., 'Knot & Vortex,'
loc.cit.

The Fixed Stars

66. DANTE, 'Paradiso,' Cantos XXII-XXVI, Divine
Comedy, op.cit.

67. POUND 'Drafts & Fragments of Cantos CX-CXVII,'
Cantos, op.cit., pp.777-802.

68. POUND, Canto CXVI, p.797.

69. POUND, 'Notes for Canto CXVII et seq.,' p.802.

70. POUND, Canto CXVI, p.795. Cf. also Canto CXIII,
p.789:
     "That Yeats noted the symbol over that portico,"
a stained glass Notre Dame over one of the porticos of
the cathedral itself (Paris).   Here is the true sense
of miniature, where the fragment INCLUDES the whole.

71. POUND, Canto CXIV, p.793.

72. POUND, Canto CX, p.781, recalling a change Pound
made in Eliot's Wasteland nearly fifty years prior.
Where   Eliot had his fragments "shelved,"   Pound
interpolated   "shored," and did the poem a great deal
of good in other ways as well. Cf. Valerie ELIOT, The
Wasteland, Facsimile Edition, New York (Harcourt,
Brace, Jovanavich) 1972.

Primum Mobile

73. DANTE, 'Paradiso,'   Cantos   XXVII-XXIX, Divine
Comedy, op.cit.

74. Omitted in early editions, Canto CXX is the final
page of The Cantos, op.cit., p.803.

75. Ibid.

76. Cf. DANTE, 'Paradiso,' Divine Comedy, op.cit.,
Canto XXVIII, lines 16-18:
     "I saw a Point of so intense a beam
          That needs must every eye it blazes on
          Be closed before its poignancy extreme."

77. F.N. ROBINSON, 'Canterbury Tales,' The Works of
Geoffrey Chaucer, 2nd Edition, Boston (Houghton,
Mifflin & Co.) 1961, p.265:
     "Heere taketh the makere of this book his leve":
     "Wherefore I biseke you mekely, for the mercy of
     God, that ye preye for me that Crist have mercy
     on me and foryeve me my giltes;/ and namely of
     my translacions and enditynges of worldly vani-
     ties, the whiche I revoke in my retracciouns..."

212

78. W.A. NEILSON & C.J. HALL, The Complete Plays and Poems of William Shakespeare, New Cambridge Edition, Boston (Houghton, Mifflin & Co.) 1942, 'The Tempest' (Shakespeare's final play), p.565, 'Epilogue, spoken by Prospero' to the audience. Prospero stands alone for the soliloquoy:

> "Now my charms are all o'erthrown,
> And what strength I have's mine own,
> Which is most faint. ...Now I want
> Spirits to enforce, art to enchant,
> And my ending is despair,
> Unless I be relieved by prayer
> Which pierces so that it assaults
> Mercy itself and frees all faults.
> As you yourself from crimes would pardoned be,
> Let your indulgence set me free."

The Rose

79. Cf. GANDILLAC, Pseudo-Denys, op.cit. Chapitres I-II.

80. DANTE, 'Paradiso,' Cantos XXX-XXXIII, Divine Comedy, op.cit. Cf. XXXIII, 133-136, where Dante likens himself, before the triune mystery, to the geometer unable to square the circle. Cf. also Figure III in the Illustrations, rhombic dodecahedron, for the resolution of this Euclidean paradox in the four-dimensional spherical cube of R.B. Fuller's synergetic geometry.

81. Beauty is for Pound order; "to kalon: order". Cf. KENNER's gloss on "beauty" in the 'Glossary' of his Bucky, op.cit., p.319: "Beauty: Unredundant appropriateness, perceived by taste."

82. "to 'see again,'/ the verb is 'see,' not 'walk on'..." Pound, Canto CXVI, p.796.

83. Cf. POUND, Spirit of Romance, op.cit., Chapter II, 'Il Miglior Fabbro.'

84. KENNER, Pound Era, op.cit., p.545: "...a poem from the Fenollosa notes to which he would not have paid attention in 1914, a poem without people in it, a poem about estranged stars... with a river -- is it the Milky Way? -- between them."

85. Both versions are reproduced on p.545 of KENNER, Pound Era, op.cit.

86. POUND, Canto 93, p.626. Cf. also POUND, Canto CXIV, p.793: "And that the truth is in kindness."

87. For example, KENNER, Pound Era, op.cit., p.377:
    "The world, he [Pound] was convinced, had once known the order it now lacked, and what has been known should not be difficult to recover, a simple matter or reactivating knowledge. And this was implicit in his guiding myth of Odysseus, whose journey through unknown dangers is directed to his former home. Mussolini seemed to be helping to rebuild Ithaca. All this (and the cage, and the madhouse) lay ahead as he assumed, in the early 1920's, the role of Odysseus and the role, simultaneously, of amanuensis for the mind of Europe, itself Odysseus, in desperate straits (wars, inflations) seeking Ithaca, questing as men always are after lost securities that lie somewhere around the rim of a great circle."

Cf. the three "great circle models" presented in our Illustrations.

88. Cf. Chapter 8.

89. In Fuller's "timeless, metaphysical" models, it can be said that not even one great circle can be intact if ALL the others are not also intact. In higher frequency models, however, one or two of the great circles may be distorted (e.g. Pound on the theme of money) without greatly damaging most of the others.

90. The "four dimensional" great circle models (WHOLES) which can be constructed from specifications provided in Fuller's Synergetics, op.cit., 'Operational Mathematics' and elsewhere, would be the real Illustrations. "Unfolding" a WHOLE enables one to get a feel for the way tensegrity systems hold together (quite startling at first) which simply cannot be conveyed in the abstract.

Illustrations: The Image As Word

1. POUND, 'I Gather the Limbs of Osiris' ('A Rather Dull Introduction'), Selected Essays of Ezra Pound, 1909-1965, op.cit., p.23.

2. POUND, Guide to Kulchur, op.cit., pp.77-8.

3. POUND, 'Medievalism,' Literary Essays, op.cit., p.154.

4. POUND, 'The Serious Artist' (1913), Literary Essays, op.cit., p.49.

5. POUND, Gaudier-Brzeska, op.cit., p.92. Pp.90-92 take mathematical generalization through stages reminiscent of his treatment of the topic in his introduction to Dante's Commedia, quoted in our Chapter 9. The passage we have cited continues:
"It is as true for the painting and the sculpture as it is for the poetry. Mr. Wadsworth and Mr. Lewis are not using words, they are using shape and colour. Mr. Brzeska and Mr. Epstein are using 'planes in relation,' they are dealing with a relation of planes different from the sort of relation of planes dealt with in geometry, hence what is called 'the need for organic forms in sculpture.'
"I trust I have made clear what I mean by an intensive art." (p.92)
Cf. Also R.B. Fuller as cited in Illustrations, b.

6. POUND, 'Brancusi,' Literary Essays, op.cit., pp.443-4. Cf. also such figures as 'Sleeping Muse,' 'Cry of the Newborn,' 'Origin of the World,' etc. in GEIST, Brancusi, Sculpture and Drawings, op.cit.

7. POUND, Gaudier-Brzeska, op.cit., p.91.

8. Ibid.

9. Pound repeatedly and emphatically refers to The Cantos as a poem including history. In Patria Mia, London (Peter Owen Ltd.) 1962, p.68, for example: "One wants to find out what sort of things endure, and what sort of things are transient; what sort of things recur; ...to learn upon what the forces, constructive or dispersive, of social order move." For Daniel PEARLMAN, Barb of Time, op.cit., time is the clue to the coherence of the whole; or at least circular, recurrent time is. It is Pearlman's thesis that the

"main theme" of The Cantos is "the unfolding of the human spirit in the medium of time."

10. R.B. FULLER, Utopia or Oblivion, New York (Overlook Press) 1969, p.76.

11. POUND's epigraph to R.B.FULLER, Intuition, New York (Doubleday/Anchor) 1973.

12. Hugh KENNER, Bucky, A Guided Tour to Buckminster Fuller, New York (Morrow) 1973, and Geodesic Math, Berkeley (UC Press) 1976. With this latter pioneering book, Kenner has added an increment of flexibility to geodesic architecture, allowing creative variations on Fuller's always-spherical domeworks. By exploring complex high-frequency geodesics, Kenner has "valved" Fuller's synergetic geometry into a spectrum of design strategies which will accommodate uniquely local applications. Our own program here is to funnel through this "vortex" of design strategies in the complementary direction, toward the simplest and most primordial "metaphysical" systems. In this way, the reader may be able to grasp some of the more universal and comprehensive articulations of "Nature's coordinate system." For cross-reference, cf. J. ARGÜELLES, Mandala, Berkeley (Shambhala) 1971.

13. In contrast to the algebra of abstraction and the overwhelming quantification of everything and anything so typical of our materialistic age. Cf. also Matila GHYKA, The Geometry of Art and Life, New York (Dover) 1977 and H.E. HUNTLEY, The Divine Proportion, A Study in Mathematical Beauty, New York (Dover) 1970.

14. R.B. FULLER & E.J. APPLEWHITE, Synergetics, op.cit., p.3.

15. Ibid., p.12.

16. Ibid., 203.08, p.24: "Synergetics makes possible the return to omniconceptual modeling of all physical intertransformations and energy-value transactions, exclusively expressed heretofore -- especially throughout the last century -- only as algebraic, nonconceptual transactions. The conceptual modeling of synergetics does not contradict but complements the exclusively algebraic expression of physical Universe relationships... The abandonment of conceptual models removed from literary men any conceptual patterns with which they might explain the evolution of scientific events to the non-mathematically-languaged public.

Ergo, the lack of modelability produced the seemingly unbridgeable social chasm between the humanities and the sciences."

17. E.J. APPLEWHITE, letter to the author, 13 June 1978.

18. FULLER & APPLEWHITE, Synergetics, op.cit., 455.11, 458.12, 450.10. Cf. also the forthcoming Unfolding Wholes, by S. EASTHAM & J. BLACKMAN.

19. POUND, Gaudier-Brzeska, op.cit., p.86.

III The Poet As Psychopomp

1. POUND, Canto XLVII, p.238.

2. Cf. Hugh Selwyn Mauberley, in POUND, Personae, op,cit., for example the lines from 'E.P. Ode Pour L'Election de Son Sepulchre' cited in note #24 of our Chapter 3, 'Vortex.'

3. POUND, Canto LXXVII, P.430; also recapitulated on pp.442 of the same Canto.

4. KENNER, Pound Era, op.cit., p.540. The communiqué is dated 11 August 1960.

5. Eliose HAY, letter to the author, 9 March 1979.

6. Cf. N. STOCK, The Life of Ezra Pound, op.cit.

7. POUND, 'The Tree,' Personae, op.cit., p.3.

8. POUND Canto CXV, p.794.

9. A common theme of R. Panikkar's. Cf., e.g., 'Sūnyāta and Plērōma, The Buddhist and Christian Response to the Human Predicament,' in PANIKKAR, The Intra-Religious Dialogue, New York (Paulist Press) 1978, p.77-100.

10. Cf. KENNER, Pound Era, op.cit., pp.485-6: "Who am I? A way of breathing. That spondee is himself. And not the least strange of the Pisan adventures was the invasion of the great dead, to speak through him and receive his signature on their cadences."

11. Cf. M. HEIDEGGER, Poetry, Language, Thought, op.cit., 'Poetically Man Dwells...', pp.221-7:
    "To write poetry is measure-taking... by which man first receives the measure for the breadth of his being... this measure gauges the very nature of man. For man dwells by spanning the "on the earth" and the "beneath the sky." This "on" and "beneath" belong together. Their interplay is that span that man traverses at every moment insofar as he is an earthly being... Because man is...his being must now and again be measured out. ...To discern this measure, to gauge it as the measure, and to accept it as the measure, means for the poet to make poetry.
    "...dwelling occurs only when poetry comes to pass and is present, and indeed...as taking a

measure for all measuring. This measure-taking
is itself an authentic measure-taking, no mere
gauging with ready-made measuring rods for the
making of maps. Nor is poetry building in the
sense of raising and fitting buildings. But
poetry, as the authentic gauging of the dimension of dwelling, is the primal form of building.
Poetry first of all admits man's dwelling into
its very nature, its presencing being. Poetry is
the original admission of dwelling."

It should be noted that this formulation of poiesis as
"measure-taking" has caused no little consternation
among Heidegger scholars. Werner MARX, in his 'Poetic
Dwelling and the Role of the Poet,' struggles with the
following questions:
    "If this is the role of the poet, however,
we must ask: Has Heidegger shown in any greater
detail how the poet assumes and realizes it? Has
Heidegger shown how a proper realization of this
role can result in a primordial, genuine and
salutary 'poetic dwelling' for the man who is not
a poet, or for all of humanity?"
(J.J. KOCKELMANS, On Heidegger & Language, op.cit.,
pp.243-4.)

12. POUND, Canto 93, p.632.

13. Cf. M. HEIDEGGER, 'The Nature of Language,' On the
Way to Language, op.cit., p.123: "The essential being
of language is Saying as Showing."

14. "Wann werten Wörter weider Wort?", as Heidegger
put it in the poem Sprache accompanying his 18 March
1976 letter to R. Panikkar's ongoing seminar on cross-
cultural religious anthropology: "When will words
become again Word?"

15. That Pound's first generation of readers -- among
them Eliot, Williams, Joyce, Hemingway and Marianne
Moore -- appropriated that milieu of creative freedom
can hardly be questioned; each did their own work
inimitably. And then Pound got them published. The
next generation of poets to fall under his sway -- the
"Objectivists" of the Depression years, Oppen, Rezni-
kov, Zukofsky and Basil Bunting -- worked with forms
of verse which would hardly even be intelligible without the context of the "Pound Era" behind them. They
were less fortunate at finding audience in their own
time. Cf. H. KENNER, A Homemade World, New York
(Knopf/Morrow) 1975. In the third generation -- one

thinks of Charles Olson's Black Mountain College pro-
geny; Duncan, Creely, Denise Levertov, Gary Snyder --
the influence is understandably more dilute, but the
impulse to "make it new" is sufficient indication of
Pound's legacy, as is the continuing effort to eschew
abstraction by discovering universals only in the
homeliest and most concrete lived human experiences.

16. The distinction between freedom to and freedom
from, as characteristic western and eastern attitudes,
is discussed in R. PANIKKAR, 'Hermeneutic of Religious
Freedom, Religion As Freedom,' the final chapter of
his Myth, Faith and Hermeneutics, op.cit. We shall
be quoting at some length from this article shortly.

17. Cf. 'Deconditioning Man,' the final section in R.
PANIKKAR, 'Śunaḥśepa, A Myth of the Human Condition,'
Myth, Faith and Hermeneutics, op.cit., pp.169-172.

18. Recall that Dante did not let Odysseus rest long
in Ithaca. Cf. DANTE, 'Inferno,' Divine Comedy,
op.cit., Canto XXVI, lines 55-143, where Ulysses tells
of his "mad venture" in quest of "the world that never
mankind has possessed," which ends when he and his
crew are swallowed up by a whirlpool after glimpsing
the Mount of Purgatory, forbidden to mortals. Cf.
also SANTILLANA & VON DECHEND, Hamlet's Mill, op.cit.,
Chapter XIV, 'The Whirlpool.' Cf. also Tennyson's
Ulysses for this incident.

19. POUND, Canto CXX, p.803.

20. POUND, Cited in KENNER, Pound Era, op.cit., p.544.
The lines were apparently written in his tower room at
Schloss Brunnenburg, circa 1962, opposite a Chinese
quatrain in his Fenollosa notes.

21. POUND, Confucius, op.cit., p.36.

EPILOGUE

1. It must be admitted that, although confined, Pound lived quite comfortably at St. Elizabeth's, entertained a continuous stream of illustrious visitors and, for once in his life, did not have to worry about making a living. As mentioned, however, one condition of his eventual release was that he be certified "incurably insane," a label within which -- for all too many would-be readers -- his life and work remain to this day confined.

2. From R. Panikkar, 'Hermeneutic of Religious Freedom,' Myth, Faith and Hermeneutics, op.cit., p.437 et seq.

3. Cf. M. de GANDILLAC, Pseudo-Denys, op.cit., 'La Hiérarchie Céleste, III, 2 (165B), p.197.

4. POUND, Canto 85, p.552.

221

BIBLIOGRAPHY

WORKS BY EZRA POUND,
in order of first publication.*

POETRY

A Lume Spento, Venice (A. Antonini) 1908. Republished,
    New York (New Directions) 1965; London (Faber &
    Faber) 1965.

A Quinzaine for this Yule, London (Pollock & Co.)
    1908; London (Elkin Mathews) 1908.

Personae, London (Elkin Mathews) 1909.

Exultations, London (Elkin Mathews) 1909. Republished
    with Personae, London (Elkin Mathews) 1909.

Provença, Boston (Small, Maynard & Co.) 1910.

Canzoni, London (Elkin Mathews) 1911. Republished
    with Ripostes, London (Elkin Mathews) 1913.

Ripostes, London (Swift & Co.) 1912. Republished,
    Boston (Small, Maynard & Co.) 1913; London (Elkin
    Mathews) 1915. Republished with Canzoni, London
    (Elkin Mathews) 1913.

Cathay, London (Elkin Mathews) 1915.

Lustra, London (Elkin Mathews) 1916. Revised edition,
    New York (Alfred Knopf) 1917.

The Fourth Canto, London (The Ovid Press) 1919.

Quia Pauper Amavi, London (The Egoist, Ltd.) 1919.
    Contains 'Three Cantos' and 'Homage to Sextus
    Propertius,' the latter republished, London (Faber
    & Faber) 1934.

Hugh Selwyn Mauberley, London (The Ovid Press) 1920.
    Reprinted in Poems 1918-1921, New York (Boni &
    Liveright) 1921, in Personae (1926), and later
    collections.

Umbra, London (Elkin Mathews) 1920.

Poems 1918-1921, New York (Boni & Liveright) 1921.

*Adapted and slightly expanded from C. BROOKE-ROSE, A
    ZBC of Ezra Pound, op.cit.

A Draft of XVI Cantos, Paris (Three Mountains Press) 1925

Personae: The Collected Poems of Ezra Pound, New York
(Boni & Liveright) 1926. Offset edition, New
York (New Directions) 1949; London (Faber &
Faber) 1952. Second edition, enlarged and
retitled, Ezra Pound -- The Collected Shorter
Poems, London (Faber & Faber) 1968.

Selected Poems, selected and introduced by T.S. Eliot,
London (Faber & Gwyer) 1928.

A Draft of XXX Cantos, Paris (Hours Press) 1930.
Republished, New York (Farrar & Rinehart) 1933;
London (Faber & Faber) 1933.

Eleven New Cantos XXXI - XLI, New York (Farrar &
Rinehart) 1934. Republished, Norfolk, Conn. (New
Directions) 1940.

Homage to Sextus Propertius, first published in Quia
Pauper Amavi, 1919; republished London (Faber &
Faber) 1934.

Alfred Venison's Poems: Social Credit Themes by the
Poet of Tichfield Street E.P., London (Stanley
Nott) 1935.

The Fifth Decad of the Cantos XLII - LI, London
(Faber & Faber) 1937; New York & Toronto (Farrar
& Rinehart) 1937; Norfolk, Conn. (New Directions)
1940.

Cantos LII -LXXI, London (Faber & Faber) 1940;
Norfolk, Conn. (New Directions) 1940.

A Selection of Poems, London (Faber & Faber) 1940.

The Pisan Cantos (LXXIV - LXXXIV), New York (New
Directions) 1948; London (Faber & Faber) 1949.

The Cantos (I - LXXXIV), New York (New Directions)
1948; London (Faber & Faber) 1954.

Selected Poems, New York (New Directions) 1949, 1957.

The Translations of Ezra Pound, Introduction by Hugh
Kenner, London (Faber & Faber) 1953, 1963; New
York (New Directions) 1953, 1963; Faber Paper-
back, 1971.

The Classic Anthology Defined by Confucius, translated
    by Ezra Pound, Cambridge, Mass. (Harvard Univer-
    sity Press) 1954; London (Faber & Faber) 1955.
    Republished as The Confucian Odes: The Classic
    Anthology Defined by Confucius, New York (New
    Directions) 1959.

Section: Rock-Drill, 85-95 de los cantares, Milano
    (All'Insegna del Pesce d'Oro) 1955; Offset edi-
    tion, New York (New Directions) 1956, London
    (Faber & Faber) 1957.

Sophokles: Women of Trachis, a version by Ezra Pound,
    London (Neville Spearman) 1956; Offset edition,
    New York (New Directions) 1957.

Diptych Rome - London: Homage to Sextus Propertius and
    Hugh Selwyn Mauberley, New York (New Directions)
    1958.

Versi prosaici, Roma (Salvatore Sciascia Editore,
    Caltanisetta) 1959. Fragments not in Cantos.

Thrones: 96 - 109 de los cantares, Milano (All'Insegna
    del Pesce d'Oro) 1959; Offset edition, New York
    (New Directions) 1959, London (Faber & Faber)
    1960.

Love Poems of Ancient Egypt, translated by Ezra Pound
    and Noel Stock, from Italian versions by Boris de
    Rachewiltz, Norfolk, Conn. (New Directions) 1962.

The Cantos of Ezra Pound I - CIX, London (Faber &
    Faber) 1964; New York (New Directions) 1965.

Canto CX, Cambridge, Mass. (Sextant Press) 1965, 80
    copies.

The Fragments (Cantos CX - CXVIII), New York (New
    Directions) 1969; London (Faber & Faber) 1970.

The Cantos of Ezra Pound, I - CXVII et seq., New York
    (New Directions) 1970. Earlier edition revised
    to include The Fragments (1970).

PROSE

The Spirit of Romance, London (Dent & Son) 1910; New York (E.P. Dutton & Co.) 1910. New edition with revisions, London (Peter Owen) 1959; Norfolk, Conn. (New Directions) 1959.

Gaudier-Brzeska: A Memoir, London (Bodley Head) 1916; New York (John Lane Co.) 1916. Reprinted, London (Laidlaw & Laidlaw) 1939. New edition with additional material, Yorks, England (The Marvell Press) 1960; New York (New Directions) 1961.

Certain Noble Plays of Japan: from the manuscripts of Ernest Fenollosa, Selected and edited by Pound, Introduction by W.B. Yeats, Churchtown, Ireland (The Cuala Press) 1916. Reprinted without Introduction as 'Noh' or Accomplishment.

'Noh' or Accomplishment, by Ernest Fenollosa and Pound, London (Macmillan & Co.) 1916; New York (Alfred Knopf) 1917. Republished as The Classic Noh Theatre of Japan, New York (New Directions) 1959.

Dialogues of Fontenelle, translated by Pound, London (The Egoist Press) 1917; London (Laidlaw & Laidlaw) 1939. Reprinted in Pavannes and Divagations (1918, 1958).

Pavannes and Divagations, New York (Alfred Knopf) 1918.

Instigations, together with The Chinese Written Character as a Medium for Poetry (Fenollosa, ed. Pound), New York (Boni & Liveright) 1920; London (Faber & Faber) 1967.

The Natural Philosophy of Love, by Remy de Gourmont, translated with Introduction by Pound, New York (Boni & Liveright) 1922; London (The Casanova Society) 1926; London (Neville Spearman) 1957.

Indiscretions; or, Une revue de deux mondes, Paris (Three Mountains Press) 1923.

The Call of the Road, by Edouard Estaunie, translated by Hiram Janus [E.P.], New York (Boni & Liveright) 1923.

Antheil or the Treatise on Harmony, Paris (Three Moun-
tains Press) 1924; Chicago (Pascal Covici) 1927.
Republished with Patria Mia as Patria Mia and The
Treatise on Harmony, London (Peter Owen) 1962.

Ta Hio, The Great Learning, an American version by
E.P., Seattle (University of Washington) 1928;
London (Stanley Nott) 1936.

Imaginary Letters, Parks (The Black Sun Press) 1930.
Reprinted in Pavannes and Divagations (1958).

How to Read, London (Desmond Harmsworth) 1931. Reprinted in Polite Essays (1937) and Literary
Essays (1954).

ABC of Economics, London (Faber & Faber) 1933; Norfolk, Conn. (New Directions) 1940; Tunbridge
Wells (Peter Russell, The Pound Press) 1953.

ABC of Reading, London (Routledge & Sons) 1934; New
Haven, Conn. (Yale University Press) 1934. Faber
Paperback, London, 1951.

Make It New, London (Faber & Faber) 1934; Offset
edition, New Haven, Conn. (Yale University Press)
1935.

Social Credit: An Impact, London (Stanley Nott) 1935.

Jefferson and/or Mussolini, London (Stanley Nott)
1935; New York (Liveright Publishing Corp.) 1936.

Confucius. Digest of the Analects, Milano (Giovanni
Scheiwiller) 1937. Reprinted in Guide to Kulchur
(1938).

Polite Essays, London (Faber & Faber) 1937; Norfolk,
Conn. (New Directions) 1940.

Guide to Kulchur, London (Faber & Faber) 1938. As
Culture, Norfolk, Conn. (New Directions) 1938;
new edition with 'Addenda 1952', London (Peter
Owen) 1952, Norfolk, Conn. (New Directions) 1952.

What is Money For?, London (Greater Britain Publica-
tions) 1939.

Italy's Policy of Social Economics 1939/40 by Odon
Por, translated by Pound, Bergamo, Milano, Roma
(Istituto Italiano d'Arti Grafiche) 1941.

Carta da Visita di Ezra Pound, Roma (Edizioni di
    Lettere d'Oggi) 1942.

L'America, Roosevelt e le cause della guerra presente,
    Venezia (Casa Editrice delle Edizioni Popolari)
    1944.

Oro e lavoro, Rapallo (Tip. Moderna) 1944.

Introduzione alla natura economica degli S.U.A., Vene-
    zia (Casa Editrice delle Edizioni Popolari) 1944.

Confucius. The Unwobbling Pivot & The Great Digest, a
    version by Ezra Pound, Pharos, No. 4, Norfolk,
    Conn. (New Directions) Winter, 1947.

If This Be Treason, Siena (printed for Olga Rudge by
    Tip. Nuova) 1948.

Patria Mia, Chicago (Ralph Fletcher Seymour) 1950.
    Written circa 1912. Reprinted with The Treatise
    on Harmony, London (Peter Owen) 1962.

The Letters of Ezra Pound 1907 - 1941, ed. D.D. Paige,
    New York (Harcourt, Brace & Co.) 1950, London
    (Faber & Faber) 1951.

Confucian Analects, a version by Ezra Pound, New York
    (Square Dollar Series) 1951; London (Peter Owen)
    1956.

Literary Essays of Ezra Pound, selected and introduced
    by T.S. Eliot, London (Faber & Faber) 1954; Nor-
    folk, Conn. (New Directions) 1954. Faber Paper-
    back, London 1960.

Pavannes and Divagations, Norfolk, Conn. (New
    Directions) 1958; Offset edition, London (Peter
    Owen) 1960. Prose and poems, mostly from earlier
    work.

Impact: Essays on Ignorance and the Decline of Ameri-
    can Civilization, by Ezra Pound, selected and
    introduced by Noel Stock, Chicago (Henry Regnery)
    1960. Includes English translations of all the
    Italian money pamphlets mentioned supra.

EP to LU: Nine Letters Written to Louis Untermeyer by
    Ezra Pound, edited by J.A. Robbins, Bloomington
    (Indiana University Press) 1963.

Confucius to Cummings, An Anthology of Poetry edited by Ezra Pound and Marcella Spann, New York (New Directions) 1964.

Confucius: The Great Digest, The Unwobbling Pivot, The Analects, translated by Ezra Pound, New York (New Directions) 1969.

Pound/Joyce -- The Letters of Ezra Pound to James Joyce, edited by Forrest Read, London (Faber & Faber) 1968,

The Chinese Written Character as a Medium for Poetry, by Ernest Fenollosa, edited by Ezra Pound, San Francisco (City Lights) 1969.

Ezra Pound, Selected Essays 1909 - 1965, New York (New Directions) 1973.

WORKS ABOUT EZRA POUND
in alphabetical order.

Baumann, Walter, The Rose in the Steel Dust: An
    Examination of the Cantos of Ezra Pound, Bern
    (Francke Verlag) 1967.

Brooke-Rose, Christine, A ZBC of Ezra Pound, Berkeley
    (University of California Press) 1971.

Cornell, Julien, The Trial of Ezra Pound: A Documented
    Account of the Treason Case by the Defendant's
    Lawyer, New York (John Day Co.) 1966.

Davie, Donald, Ezra Pound, Poet as Sculptor, New York
    (Oxford University Press) 1964; London (Routledge)
    1965.

    Ezra Pound, New York (Viking) 1975.

Davis, Earle, Vision fugitive: Ezra Pound and Econo-
    mics, Lawrence, Kansas (University of Kansas
    Press) 1969.

Dekker, George, Sailing after Knowledge, The Cantos of
    Ezra Pound, A Critical Appraisal, London
    (Routledge) 1963; New York (Barnes & Noble) 1963.

Dembo, Lawrence Sanford, The Confucian Odes of Ezra
    Pound, A Critical Appraisal, London (Faber &
    Faber) 1963; Berkeley (University of California
    Press) 1963.

Edwards, John Hamilton, and Vasse, William V., The
    Annotated Index to the Cantos I - LXXXIV, Berkeley
    (University of California Press) 1957.

Emery, Clark, Ideas into Action, A Study of Pound's
    Cantos, Coral Gables, Florida (University of
    Miami Press) 1958.

Espey, John J., Ezra Pound's Mauberley: A Study in
    Composition, Berkeley (University of California
    Press) 1955; London (Faber & Faber) 1955.

Fraser, G.S., Ezra Pound, London (Oliver & Boyd) 1960;
    New York (Grove Press) 1961.

Gallup, Donald, A Bibliography of Ezra Pound, London (Rupert Hart-Davis) 1963, 1966.

Goodwin, K.L. The Influence of Ezra Pound, London (Oxford University Press) 1966.

Hesse, Eva (Ed.), New Approaches to Ezra Pound, London (Faber & Faber) 1969; Berkeley (University of California Press) 1969.

Heymann, D., The Last Rower, Berkeley (University of California Press) 1976.

Hutchins, Patricia, Ezra Pound's Kensington, An Exploration 1885-1913, London (Faber & Faber) 1965.

Jackson, Thomas H., The Early Poetry of Ezra Pound, Cambridge, Mass. (Harvard University Press) 1969; London (Oxford University Press) 1969.

Kenner, Hugh, The Poetry of Ezra Pound, London (Faber & Faber) 1951; New York (New Directions) 1951.

The Pound Era, Berkeley (University of California Press) 1971.

Leary, Lewis (Ed.), Motive and Method in the Cantos of Ezra Pound, New York (Columbia University Press) 1954.

Mullins, Eustace Clarence, This Difficult Individual, Ezra Pound, New York (Fleet Publishing Corp.) 1961.

de Nagy, N. Christoph, The Poetry of Ezra Pound: The Pre-Imagist Stage, Bern (Francke Verlag) 1960.

Ezra Pound's Poetics and Literary Tradition: The Critical Decade, Bern (Francke Verlag) 1966.

Norman, Charles, The Case of Ezra Pound, New York (Macmillan) 1960.

Ezra Pound, A Biography, London (Macdonald) 1969.

O'Connor, William Van, and Stone, Edward, A Casebook on Ezra Pound, New York (Crowell) 1959.

Pearlman, Daniel S., The Barb of Time, London and New York (Oxford University Press) 1969.

Perloff, Marjorie, The Poetics of Indeterminacy: From Rimbaud to Cage, New Jersey (Princeton) 1982.

de Rachewiltz, Marie, Discretions, New York (Atlantic/ Little, Brown, Inc.) 1971.

Rosenthal, M.L., A Primer of Ezra Pound, New York (Macmillan) 1960.

de Roux, Dominique (Ed.), Ezra Pound, Paris (Les Cahiers de l'Herne) 1965, 1966, in two vols.

Russell, Peter, Ezra Pound: A Collection of Essays to be Presented to Ezra Pound on his 65th Birthday, London (Peter Nevill) 1950; and under the title An Examination of Ezra Pound: A Collection of Essays, New York (New Directions) 1950.

Ruthven, K.K., A Guide to Ezra Pound's "Personae" (1926), Berkeley (University of California Press) 1968.

San Juan, E., Jr., (Ed.), Critics on Ezra Pound, Miami (University of Miami Press) 1972.

Schneidau, Herbert N., Ezra Pound: The Image and the Real, Baton Rouge (Louisiana State University Press) 1969.

Stock, Noel, Poet in Exile: Ezra Pound, Manchester (Manchester University Press) 1964; New York (Barnes & Noble) 1964.

(Ed.) Ezra Pound: Perspectives, Chicago (Henry Regnery) 1965.

Reading the Cantos: A Study of Meaning in Ezra Pound, London (Routledge) 1967.

The Life of Ezra Pound, London (Routledge & Kegan Paul) 1970.

Sullivan, J.P., Ezra Pound and Sextus Propertius, A Study in Creative Translation, Austin (University of Texas Press) 1964; London (Faber & Faber) 1964.

Sutton, Walter (Ed.), Ezra Pound: A Collection of Critical Essays, Eaglewood Cliffs, NJ (Prentice-Hall) 1963.

Watts, Harold H., Ezra Pound and the Cantos, Chicago (Henry Regnery) 1952.

Wilhelm, James, The Later Cantos of Ezra Pound, New York (Walker & Walker) 1977.

Yeats, W.B., A Vision, New York/London (Macmillan) 1937.

OTHER SOURCES

Anderson, William, trans., Dante, The New Life, New
    York (Penguin) 1964.

Argüelles, José, The Transformative Vision, Berkeley
    (Shambhala) 1975.

    Mandala, Berkeley (Shambhala) 1971.

Barthes, Roland, Elements of Semiology, London (Cape)
    1967.

Belford, Lee A., (Ed.), Religious Dimensions in Litera-
    ture, New York (Seabury) 1982.

Bernstein, J.M. (Ed.), Baudelaire, Rimbaud, Verlaine,
    New York (Citadel) 1965.

Binyon, Laurence, trans., The Divine Comedy, in Mila-
    no, P., The Portable Dante, New York (Viking)
    1947.

Brown, Norman O, Love's Body, New York (Vintage) 1966.

    Hermes the Thief, The Evolution of a Myth, New
    York (Vintage) 1969.

    Closing Time, New York (Vintage) 1973.

Butterworth, E.A.S., The Tree at the Navel of the
    Earth, Berlin (Walter De Gruyter & Co.) 1970.

Campbell, Joseph, Masks of God, Vol. I, Primitive
    Mythology, New York (Vintage) 1959.

de Chardin, Teilhard, The Phenomenon of Man, New York
    (Harper & Row) 1959.

    The Future of Man, New York (Harper & Row) 1964.

    Building the Earth, New York (Dimension Books)
    1965.

Conybeare, F.C., trans., Philostratus' Life of Apol-
    lonius of Tyana, New York (Macmillan) 1912.

Corbin, Henry, Creative Imagination in the Sufism of
    Ibn 'Arabi, R. Manheim translation, Princeton,
    (Bollingen) 1969.

234

Eliade, Mircea, <u>Shamanism</u>, Princeton (Bollingen) 1972.

    <u>Yoga -- Immortality and Freedom</u>, Princeton (Bollingen) 1958.

    <u>Cosmos and History</u>, New York (Harper Torchbooks) 1959.

    <u>The Sacred and the Profane</u>, New York (Harvest Books) 1959.

    <u>Myth, Dreams & Mysteries</u>, London (Fontana Library) 1968.

Eliot, T.S. <u>Four Quartets</u>, New York (Harvest Books) 1971.

Eliot, Valerie (Ed.), <u>T.S. Eliot, The Wasteland</u> (Facsimile Edition), New York (Harvest Books) 1971.

Erickson, E., Jr., (Ed.) <u>Religion and Modern Literature: Essays in Theory and Criticism</u>, Grand Rapids (Eerdmans) 1975.

Feldman & Richardson, <u>The Rise of Modern Mythology</u>, Bloomington (Indiana University Press) 1972.

Fingarette, H. <u>Confucius -- The Secular As Sacred</u>, New York (Harper & Row) 1972.

Fuller, R. Buckminster, <u>Intuition</u>, New York (Anchor) 1973.

    <u>Utopia or Oblivion</u>, New York (Overlook) 1969.

    <u>Operating Manual for Spaceship Earth</u>, New York (Pocket Books) 1970.

    <u>No More Secondhand God</u>, New York (Anchor) 1971.

Fuller, R.B. and Applewhite, E.J., <u>Synergetics--Explorations in the Geometry of Thinking</u>, New York (Macmillan) 1975, 1979.

Fung, Y.L., <u>A History of Chinese Philosophy</u>, D. Bodde trans., Vol. I., Princeton (Bollingen) 1952.

Gadamer, Hans-Georg, <u>Truth and Method</u>, New York (Seabury) 1976.

de Gandillac, Maurice (Trans.,) Oeuvres Complètes du Pseudo-Denys L'Aréopagite, Paris (Aubier) 1943.

Geist, Sidney, Brancusi, The Sculpture and Drawings, New York (Harry N. Abrams, Inc.) 1975.

Ghyka, Matila, The Geometry of Art and Life, New York (Dover) 1977.

Goichon, A.M., trans., Avicenna, La Récit de Hayy Ibn Yaqzān, Paris (Desclée de Broumer) 1959.

Graves, Robert, The White Goddess, New York (Noonday Press) 1969.

Gunn, Giles, ed., Religion and Literature, London (SCM Press Ltd.) 1971.

Halifax, Joan, Shamanic Voices, New York (E.P. Dutton) 1979.

Harrison, Jane Ellen, Themis, New York (World) 1912, 1927.

Heidegger, Martin, Poetry, Language, Thought, A. Hofstadter, trans., New York (Harper & Row) 1971.

On the Way to Language, P.D. Hertz, trans., New York (Harper & Row) 1971.

Existence and Being, W. Brock (Ed.), Chicago (Henry Regnery) 1949.

What is Called Thinking?, Wieck and Gray trans., New York (Harper & Row) 1972.

Identity and Difference, Joan Stambaugh, trans., New York (Harper & Row) 1969.

Hopper, S.R., (Ed.), Interpretation: The Poetry of Meaning, New York (Harcourt, Brace & World) 1967.

Huntley, H.E., The Divine Proportion, A Study in Mathematical Beauty, New York (Dover) 1970.

James, William, The Varieties of Religious Experience, New York (New American Library) 1958.

Joyce, James, Ulysses, New York (Random House) 1934.

Finnegans Wake, New York (Viking) 1967.

Jung, Carl Gustav, Psychology and Alchemy, Princeton
(Bollingen) 1958. Vol. 12 of Collected Works.

Psychology and Religion: West and East, Princeton
(Bollingen) 1958. Vol. 11 of Collected Works.

The Spirit in Man, Art, and Literature, Princeton
(Bollingen) 1966. Vol. 15 of Collected Works.

The Undiscovered Self, R.F.C. Hull, trans.,
Collected, Boston (Atlantic - Little, Brown)
1957.

Jung, C.G. and Kerenyi, C., Essays on a Science of
Mythology, Princeton (Bollingen) 1963.

Jung, C.G. and Wilhelm, R., The Secret of the Golden
Flower, New York (Harcourt, Brace & World) 1962.

Kazantzakis, Nikos, The Odyssey, A Modern Sequel, K.
Friar, trans., New York (Simon & Schuster) 1958.

Kenner, Hugh, Bucky, A Guided Tour of Buckminster
Fuller, New York (Morrow) 1973.

A Homemade World, New York (Morrow) 1975.

Geodesic Math, and how to use it, Berkeley
(University of California Press) 1976.

Kocklemans, J.J. (Ed.), On Heidegger and Language,
Evanston (Northwestern University Press) 1972.

Larsen, Stephen, The Shaman's Doorway, New York (Harper & Row) 1976.

Lattimore, Richmond, trans., The Odyssey of Homer, New
York (Harper & Row) 1965.

Levi-Strauss, Claude, The Savage Mind, Chicago
(University of Chicago Press) 1966.

The Raw and the Cooked, Introduction to a
Science of Mythology, New York (Harper & Row)
1969.

Levy, G.R., The Gate of Horn, London (Faber &
Faber) 1963.

Liu, Wu-Chi, A Short History of Confucian
Philosophy, New York (Delta) 1964.

237

McClain, Ernest, The Myth of Invariance, Boulder (Shambhala) 1978.

Murray, Michael, (Ed.), Heidegger & Modern Philosophy, New Haven (Yale University Press) 1978.

Needham, J., Science and Civilization in China, Cambridge (Cambridge University Press) 1956.

Neihart, John G., Black Elk Speaks, Lincoln (University of Nebraska Press) 1961.

Neilson, W.A., & C.J. Hall, The Complete Plays and Poems of William Shakespeare, New Cambridge Edition, Boston (Houghton, Mifflin & Co.) 1942.

Neuman, Erich, The Great Mother, Princeton (Bollingen) 1955.

Art and the Creative Unconsicous, Princeton (Bollingen) 1959.

Ortega y Gasset, José, What is Philosophy?, New York (Norton Library) 1960.

The Dehumanization of Art, Princeton, NJ (Princeton University Press) 1968.

Panikkar, Raimundo, The Trinity and the Religious Experience of Man, New York (Orbis Books) 1973.

The Intra-Religious Dialogue, New York (Paulist) 1978.

Myth, Faith & Hermeneutics, New York (Paulist) 1979.

'Colligite Fragmenta: Toward An Integration of Reality,' in From Alienation to At-Oneness, Proceedings of the Theology Institute, Villanova University, 1977.

Le Mystère du Culte dans l'Hindouisme et l'Christianisme, Paris (Editions du Cerf) 1970.

The Vedic Experience, Berkeley (University of California Press) 1977.

El Silencio Del Dios, Madrid (Tiempo al tiempo)
1970.

Reichard, Gladys A., Navajo Religion, Princeton
(Bollingen) 1963.

Richardson, William J., S.J., Heidegger - Through
Phenomenology to Thought, The Hague (Martinus
Nijhoff) 1963.

Ricoeur, Paul, The Rule of the Metaphor, Multidisciplinary Studies of the Creation of Meaning in
Language, Toronto (University of Toronto Press)
1978.

'Parole et Symbole,' in Le Symbole, Strasbourg
(Faculté de Theologie Catholique, Palais
Universitaire) 1975, pp. 142-161.

Rilke, R.M., The Duino Elegies, Garmey & Wilson
trans., New York (Harper & Row) 1972.

Sonnets to Orpheus, M.D.H. Norton, trans., New
York (Norton Library) 1970.

Robinson, F.N. (Ed.), 'Canterbury Tales,' The Works
of Geoffrey Chaucer, 2nd Edition, Boston
(Houghton, Mifflin & Co.) 1961.

Rohde, Erwin, Psyche, The Cult of Souls and Belief
in Immortality among the Greeks, Vols. I and
II, W.C. Guthrie trans., New York (Harper &
Row) 1966.

Rolt, C.E., trans., Dionysus the Areopagite, Divine
Names and Mystical Theology, London (SPCK) 1971.

Sanders, N.K., The Epic of Gilgamesh, Baltimore
(Penguin) 1960.

de Santillana, G., and von Dechend, H., Hamlet's
Mill, Boston (Godine) 1977.

Scott, Nathan, The Broken Center, New Haven &
London (Yale University Press), 1966.

Sinclair, John D., The Divine Comedy of Dante
Alighieri: III 'Paradiso', New York (Oxford)
1939.

Smith, Logan Pearsall, The English Language, London (Oxford) 1966.

Steiner, George, After Babel, Aspects of Language and Translation, London (Oxford) 1975.

Stevenson, W.T., History as Myth, New York (Seabury) 1969.

Thomas, Lewis, Lives of A Cell, New York (Viking) 1974.

Untermeyer, Lewis (Ed.), Modern American and Modern British Poetry, New York (Harcourt, Brace & World) 1955.

Upward, Allen, The Divine Mystery, Letchworth (Garden City Press) 1913; re-released, Santa Barbara (Ross-Erikson, Inc.) 1976.

Waley, Arthur, The Analects of Confucius, New York (Random House) 1938.

Wilder, Amos, The New Voice, New York (Herder & Herder) 1969.

Wilhelm, Richard, Confucius and Confucianism, New York (Harvest Books) 1931.

Williams, W.C., Paterson, New York (New Directions) 1963.

Pictures From Brueghel and other poems, New York (New Directions) 1955.

Selected Poems, New York (New Directions) 1949.

Yeats, W.B., Collected Poems, New York (Macmillan) 1956.

***

finis

ABOUT THE AUTHOR

Born in Chicago, 1949, with a Ph.D. in Religious
Studies from the University of California, Scott
Eastham is currently Assistant Professor of Religion
and Religious Education at The Catholic University
of America in Washington, D.C. As evidenced by
this book, his focal concerns in teaching and research are Religion and Culture, Religion and Literature, and Cross-Cultural Religious Anthropology.